EDINBURGH: SCIENNES AND THE GRANGE

To my son
Graham
To complete the family dedications
Game, set and match

EDINBURGH: SCIENNES AND THE GRANGE

MALCOLM CANT

Foreword by
Professor DAVID DAICHES

JOHN DONALD PUBLISHERS LTD
EDINBURGH

ISBN 0 85976 253 X

British Library Cataloguing in Publication Data
Cant, Malcolm
Edinburgh: Sciennes and the Grange
1. Edinburgh, history
I. Title
941.34

Phototypeset by Pioneer Associates, Perthshire
Printed and Bound in Great Britain by
Bell & Bain Ltd., Glasgow.

FOREWORD

We are accustomed to think of Edinburgh's Old Town and the Royal Mile as the real centres of historical interest for those concerned with the city. But many other areas of Edinburgh are rich in history, and Sciennes and the Grange are notably so. Malcolm Cant has researched his material well and tells the story of people, buildings, streets and institutions in this area over the centuries. It is a rich and absorbing story. For those who like myself grew up in this part of Edinburgh it is fascinating to be able to trace the past of places one has known intimately. Cities have their memories as well as people, and without cultivating that memory a city risks losing its character. This book contributes richly to Edinburgh's knowledge of itself.

David Daiches

ACKNOWLEDGEMENTS

The more I research the City of Edinburgh, the more I come to the conclusion that there are countless books waiting to be written from the vast quantity of archival material held in the many institutions and libraries throughout the City. They have all been of great value to me in writing *Edinburgh: Sciennes and the Grange* including the Cockburn Association; the Company of Merchants of the City of Edinburgh; Edinburgh City Archivist; Edinburgh University Library; National Library of Scotland; Royal College of Physicians; Royal College of Surgeons; Royal Commission on the Ancient and Historical Monuments of Scotland; Royal Incorporation of Architects in Scotland; Royal Society of Edinburgh; Scotsman Publications Ltd; Scottish Record Office; Signet Library. Without the constant assistance of the staff, my task would not have been accomplished.

In the chapter devoted to churches I was fortunate to have assistance from the Rev. Ian A. Dunlop who had only just completed his own invaluable work, *The Kirks of Edinburgh*. Six churches came within the area of my research. I wish to thank the respective ministers and members of the congregations, who contributed to my understanding of these churches: Marchmont St. Giles, the Rev. Donald M. Stephen; Reid Memorial, the Rev. B. M. Embleton and Malcolm Anderson; St. Catherine's Argyle, the Rev. Victor W. N. Laidlaw and Ed Skedd; Salisbury, the Rev. Brian C. Casebow; Mayfield, the Very Rev. W. J. G. McDonald, the Rev. Hamish McIntosh, Barbara Dodds and Ian Dodds; German Lutheran Church, Dr Hans Speitel.

When I came to study the hospitals and the Royal Dick Veterinary College the high quality of the advice given by the doctors and administrators seemed to me to far outweigh my ability to absorb it and portray it accurately for my readers. I hope I have succeeded. I thank Mr G. A. MacKinlay, Chairman of the Hospital Management Team, and others, at the Royal Hospital for Sick Children; H. R. Wedgwood of Roland Wedgwood Associates, Architects, Norman Dunhill, Joan Cairns and the Sisters of the Little Company of Mary at St. Raphael's; Dr Norman Hood at the Longmore Hospital; and Professor A. Iggo and Dr J. E. Phillips for their assistance in tracing the history and development of the Royal Dick Veterinary College.

The chapter on schools produced more information than I had expected, due no doubt to the enthusiastic response which I received to my several enquiries. I thank Dr and Mrs James Gray for inviting me to their home which was formerly occupied by the Bell Academy, also Mrs A. Wilkinson and Mrs Kathleen Biggers for their help with the Grange Home School. My script on Esdaile was enhanced by discussions with the last headmistress, Miss Margaret Ewan, and former pupils Margaret Ingram and Lynn Gladstone-Millar. The Royal Bank of Scotland also allowed me access to the former school building in Kilgraston Road. I also thank Miss M. C. Fraser and Miss E. Landells for their recollections of Craigmount Girls' School, and Alastair K. Ross for information on Margaret Kinmont Ross, the headmistress from 1932 to 1949. The story of the Trades Maiden Hospital was put together after reference to the Incorporated Trades of Edinburgh. Finally the largest school, Sciennes, produced the most comprehensive information through the assistance of Mrs M. I. Pollock, the headteacher. The extract from *H.M. Inspectors of Schools Report* is reproduced with the permission of the Controller of Her Majesty's Stationery Office.

In my final chapter, I learned a great deal about what is happening in Sciennes and the Grange today, which has not generally found its way into previous books on this area. In putting the chapter together I thank Applecross Properties Ltd., Bank of Scotland, Barnardo's, Blyth and Blyth Group, British Geological Survey, Edinburgh School of Agriculture, Faculty of Actuaries, Nature Conservancy Council, Salvation

Army, Scottish Brewery Archives, and Scottish and Newcastle Breweries.

The story of the sporting life of the Grange is confined to the history of two clubs dating from the nineteenth century. C. R. G. Paul kindly checked my information on the Carlton Cricket Club and S. Barbour on Whitehouse and Grange Bowling Club. Several persons provided me with details of particular aspects of my study, including James C. Allan, Mrs Helen Davidson, John G. Gray, Dale Idiens, Jean Smart, Douglas F. Stewart and the Paterson-Brown family. My reference to the Villa Policy in the Grange followed a discussion with several members of the Grange Association. I thank Mrs Sofia Leonard, Mrs Dorothy Ryle and Miss Caroline Fortescue, adding the important rider that, whilst I am in general agreement with the work of the Association, it should not be saddled with responsibility for my views on any part of the Grange.

I also thank Bryan Ryalls for producing the maps at the beginning of the book and Malcolm Liddle for dealing with photographic matters prior to publication. Credit for individual photographs is shown throughout the book.

I am indebted to Professor David Daiches for writing the Foreword and to John Tuckwell and others of John Donald Publishers Ltd. for bringing the project to fruition.

Morag Sinclair has again checked the proofs with great care, which I greatly appreciate.

It remains, therefore, to thank the members of my family who have all undertaken various tasks associated with the book. My wife, Phyllis, typed the script, took many of the photographs and frequently acted as a barometer — lightening the atmosphere before a depression set in!

Here, then, is the result of all this assistance to be digested according to the appetite of the individual reader. Some appetites are satisfied by the merest nibble, whilst others, once whetted, are insatiable. For myself, I always like a double helping, without, I hope, making a meal of it.

Malcolm Cant

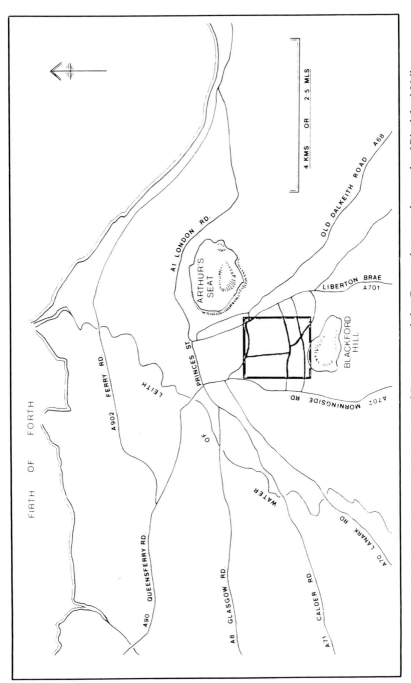

Map of Edinburgh showing the location of Sciennes and the Grange lying to the north of Blackford Hill.

x

CONTENTS

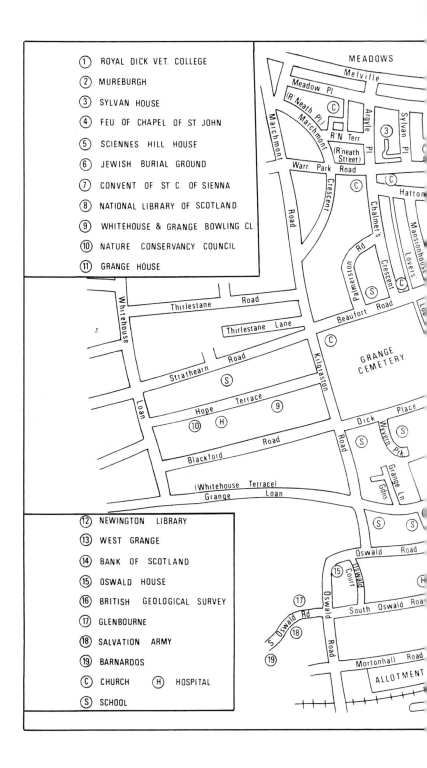

1. ROYAL DICK VET. COLLEGE
2. MUREBURGH
3. SYLVAN HOUSE
4. FEU OF CHAPEL OF ST. JOHN
5. SCIENNES HILL HOUSE
6. JEWISH BURIAL GROUND
7. CONVENT OF ST. C. OF SIENNA
8. NATIONAL LIBRARY OF SCOTLAND
9. WHITEHOUSE & GRANGE BOWLING CL.
10. NATURE CONSERVANCY COUNCIL
11. GRANGE HOUSE

12. NEWINGTON LIBRARY
13. WEST GRANGE
14. BANK OF SCOTLAND
15. OSWALD HOUSE
16. BRITISH GEOLOGICAL SURVEY
17. GLENBOURNE
18. SALVATION ARMY
19. BARNARDOS
C CHURCH   H HOSPITAL
S SCHOOL

MEADOWS
Melville
Meadow Pl
(R'neath Pl)
R'N Terr
(R'neath Street)
Argyle Pl
Sylvan Pl
Marchmont
Marchmont
Warr. Park Road
Crescent
Hatton
Chalmer's Crescent
Mansionhouse
Lovers'
Road
Palmerston Rd
GRANGE CEMETERY
Whitehouse
Thirlestane Road
Thirlestane Lane
Beaufort Road
Loe
Strathearn Road
Kilgraston
Loan
Hope Terrace
Dick Place
Blackford Road
Wyvern Prk
(Whitehouse Terrace)
Grange Loan
Grange Ln
Grange Gdns
Oswald Road
Oswald Court
Oswald Road
South Oswald Road
S Oswald Rd
Road
Mortonhall Road
ALLOTMENT

SCIENNES and
THE GRANGE

CHAPTER 1

INTRODUCTION

THE DISTRICTS OF SCIENNES AND THE GRANGE are steeped in history, and, in consequence, have been given a great deal of attention by writers on Edinburgh. Grant and Wilson devote lengthy sections to the area, and to a much lesser extent, so does Ballingall. By far the most comprehensive study is, however, *The Grange of St. Giles* by Mrs J. Stewart Smith. In more recent years, the districts have been studied and described by John G. Gray in *The South Side Story*, by Charles J. Smith in *Historic South Edinburgh*, and by the Grange Association in *The Grange – A Case for Conservation*.

In the following four chapters of *Edinburgh: Sciennes and the Grange* I have arranged the material in more or less chronological order. Thereafter, particular subjects have been dealt with separately, such as the schools, churches and hospitals. It seemed pertinent to start with the early history of the Grange, centred on Grange House, which existed well into the twentieth century. Its tragic demolition in 1936 is all the more regrettable in this age of conservation. The involvement of the early owners, Wardlaw, Cant, Dick and Lauder, is an integral part of the story, and particular attention has been given to a description of Grange House, its traditions and ghosts, and its eventual demise. The early history of Sciennes is equally interesting, based primarily on the Chapel of St. John the Baptist, the Convent of St. Catherine of Sienna and Sciennes Hill House. The mid-eighteenth century law case of Dick-Lauder of Grange v Johnstone of Westerhall also provides interesting detail on the early development of the area and the intriguing argument about the exact site of St. Catherine's Convent.

The fourth and fifth chapters trace the changes in Sciennes and the Grange in the nineteenth century as various

1

Looking north on Causewayside (later renamed Ratcliffe Terrace) at the junction with Fountainhall Road, c 1900. The buildings occupied by Ratcliffe Family Laundry and James Cochrane, Coach Hirer, were demolished to make way for the present tenements and shops. From the Yerbury Collection.

feuing plans were unfolded. The districts developed in very different ways, with Sciennes having a much closer geographical affinity with Roseneath and Argyle, which were described in my *Marchmont in Edinburgh*. For the sake of completeness, aspects of Roseneath and Argyle have been included in the chapter on the feuing of Sciennes. Additional information has also come to light on Sylvan House and the old feus which were developed for the Royal Edinburgh Hospital for Sick Children, Sciennes School and the streets of Livingstone Place and Gladstone Terrace. The feuing of the Grange, first sanctioned by a private Act of Parliament in 1825, was very closely regulated. The Act allowed Sir Thomas Dick-Lauder to feu large areas of farmland for the construction of villas, designed by many of the foremost architects of the day. Although the Grange has come under pressure from subsequent building development, it is a great credit to the original planners that so much of the character of the district has survived for almost a century and a half.

Archway built at Minto Street near the junction with Salisbury Place for the visit of King Edward VII and Queen Alexandra in 1903, the year after their Coronation. From the Yerbury Collection.

The feuing plans show how the district was eventually built up with houses of various sizes, set in extensive gardens, leaving areas of open ground for Grange Cemetery, Carlton Cricket Ground and Whitehouse and Grange Bowling Club. Various publications give some idea of the first people who lived in the Grange, many with interesting family histories of their own. Of particular significance is the story of the Buchanan family, obtained first-hand from the last surviving member of the household, who died in 1988.

In the latter part of the book three chapters deal respectively with the churches, the schools, the hospitals and the Royal Dick Veterinary College. Both Sciennes and the Grange attracted a great many churches as the population increased in the nineteenth century. The history and development of each church has been traced from its origins — often in the Old Town of Edinburgh — through the various unions, to the present day. The chapter on schools turned out to be the longest in the book, although some material has been omitted. The Grange, particularly, attracted several private schools, many of which were too small to be included. Others, however, like the Grange Home School, had high attendances for many years and continued after St. Trinnean's and Craigmount had closed their doors. The distinctive origins of the Ministers' Daughters' College, founded by Esdaile, the mesmeric doctor, and the Trades Maiden Hospital are also recorded. Two omissions require explanation: part of George Watson's College was at St. Alban's Road from 1943 to 1974 but has been included in Chapter 9 under the section on the Bank of Scotland, which acquired the premises in 1974 from the Merchant Company Education Board. The other regrettable omission, based on the absence of records, is the original Board School in Causewayside. By contrast, Sciennes School, the biggest in the district, has all its logbooks intact, ready to tell its own centenary story in 1992.

The hospitals are dealt with in Chapter 8. The oldest, and probably the best known, is the Royal Edinburgh Hospital for Sick Children which has occupied several buildings in Edinburgh, and still faces the prospect of further

Cable car 179 at Salisbury c 1905. Courtesy of D. L. G. Hunter.

expansion. The Longmore Hospital was established at Salisbury Place in 1874 and has remained there ever since, and St. Raphael's Hospital was set up at the end of the First World War to care for severely disabled ex-servicemen at Kilravock in Blackford Avenue. The chapter is concluded with a section on the Royal Dick Veterinary College, founded by William Dick in 1823 and almost in ruins seven years after his death in 1866, before rising again to its present position at the forefront of veterinary medicine.

The last chapter brings together several public and private organisations in the district at the present day. Most of these are in the Grange and many of them have been there for a very long time. The importance of the chapter is threefold: firstly, the historic significance of the buildings is recorded; secondly, a brief description is given of the nature

Edinburgh Corporation Transport 'charabanc' B8725 in West Mains Road, 1919, near the present Scottish headquarters of the British Geological Survey. Courtesy of D. L. G. Hunter.

of the work done by the organisations concerned; and thirdly (taken together), the chapter illustrates some of the reasons for the interest in the future use of the larger private dwellings. Each of these three points requires further explanation. On the first point it would be interesting, but not practical, to trace the previous ownership of almost every house in the district. Space permits only a few, but those selected reveal individual points of importance, for example, the group of houses at the west end of South Oswald Road included Blackford Park, built as the home of Andrew Usher who gifted money to the City for the Usher Hall in Lothian Road. Secondly, details of the work done by these organ-

Changing shifts on points duty at the junction of Salisbury Road and Minto Street in the early 1930s. On the left is P.C. Alexander Norrie and on the right is P.C. John Kennell. The vehicle in the background is a taxi at the Salisbury Road stance, which was originally used by horse-drawn cabs. Courtesy of Mrs Helen Davidson (née Norrie).

isations have been included which, I hope, give a brief understanding of their position in the community, such as the National Library of Scotland at Causewayside, the British Geological Survey in Grange Terrace, and the Nature Conservancy Council in Hope Terrace. The third point is more controversial in the sense that it calls into question whether private houses in the Grange should be altered to non-residential use. The gradual invasion of non-residential uses threatens to erode the essential character of the Grange which merited statutory protection in 1983 and the Grange Association feels that it should be strongly resisted. Of the few houses selected for study here, some interesting facts emerge. The three large detached houses, built in the late 1870s in St. Alban's Road, and used by the Bank of Scotland for their Training Department since 1974, ceased to be in private occupation in the early 1950s, and one was occupied as a school as early as 1891. South Park, built in Grange Terrace in 1876, ceased to be a private house in 1928, when it was purchased by the Geological Survey, and Blackford Brae, also dating from the 1870s, became a residential home for Barnardos in 1945. By contrast, many equally grand houses, which were not acquired for non-residential use, were demolished and replaced by modern flats, for example, Ashfield and West Grange in Grange Loan, Monkwood in Kilgraston Road and Mount Grange in Hope Terrace — to say nothing of Grange House itself. Which is better — Grange House, beautifully restored and maintained, say, as the headquarters of some Scottish company, or two Wyvern pillars, and a handful of stones in Huntly House Museum? Unfortunately, the answer is not quite as simple as it might appear. In fact, it is part of a much wider problem which has occupied the minds of the Planning Department and the Grange Association for several years, i.e. how to allow the Grange to develop, whilst maintaining the character of its streets and houses, including the walls, gates, pillars and garden ground. After nearly eight years of relentless pressure from the Grange Association in defence of the gardens as part and parcel of the 'Special Character' of the Conservation Area, which it is desirable to preserve and enhance, the Planning Department of the District Council finally adopted a Villa Policy in 1989, to apply to the Grange and other nineteenth-century villa areas of Edinburgh. This policy, which includes important new criteria, is largely based on

A pleasing example of the many stone-built family villas of the Grange, constructed in Lauder Road around 1879. Photograph by Phyllis M. Cant.

the Grange Report of 1982. It regulates new building in garden ground: villas are to remain substantially as they are, with subdivision into smaller units preferable to demolition; all new building or alterations should be with materials in sympathy with the existing buildings in the immediate area; and important new rules regarding the ratio of the building size to the total garden ground must be adhered to. The implementation of this Villa Policy should prevent the spread of unsympathetic infill of garden ground with buildings which are either too big for the site or not in the same style, or materials, as the adjacent houses. Subdivision of larger houses is still a viable alternative provided the external appearance of the building is unaffected and the interior features are retained as far as is practicable. A good example of this is Carrington House in South Oswald Road which was skilfully divided into five flats in 1953 by Grange (Edinburgh) Heritable Investment Company. The whole of the exterior stonework was retained along with the magnificent mahogany staircase, stained-glass windows, friezes and a variety of well proportioned rooms.

Fortunately the same problems have not been experienced in Sciennes. Most of Sciennes was developed as tenement flats, many of which have benefited from recent renovation of stonework and services. The relationship between residential and non-residential use is, in fact, the reverse of that in the Grange. Various businesses, notably Bertrams, have disappeared from Sciennes, allowing the sites to be developed for housing, and there are virtually no open spaces vulnerable to unwelcome development.

CHAPTER 2

THE EARLY HISTORY OF THE GRANGE

THE EARLY HISTORY OF THE GRANGE is closely linked with Grange House, set in what was originally the farm or Grange of St. Giles, dating from the twelfth century. By the fourteenth century the lands of Grange were in secular hands, firstly the Wardlaw family and then through the Cants to the Dicks and the Lauders. It is a fascinating history, of both local and national importance, interrupted by periods of extreme tragedy. Grange House was visited by Bonnie Prince Charlie in 1745 and became a Mecca for Edinburgh literati in the days of Sir Thomas Dick-Lauder. It was Sir Thomas who commissioned W. H. Playfair in 1827 to transform the old Scottish keep into an elegant baronial mansion. Despite the enormous sum of money spent on the Playfair plans the house was almost ruinous a century later, and was demolished in 1936.

Although Grange House has not been in existence for the last fifty years, its history still makes a significant impact on the character of the neighbourhood, whose streets are all named after the families of Dick, Lauder, Seton and Cumin.

SANCT GEILLIE – GRANGE

IT IS NOT KNOWN who built Grange House, nor the year of its construction, but there are several dates in the early twelfth century which give an indication of its origin. This early history is reviewed in detail by Mrs J. Stewart Smith in *The Grange of St. Giles*. Around 1112 Alexander I (1106–1124) erected a new Parish Kirk in Edinburgh which he dedicated to St. Giles. His successor David I (1124–1153) conferred the lands of Grange in 1128 on the monks of Holme Cultram near Carlisle, Cumberland at that time being in the possession of the Scottish King. It seems likely, therefore, that some time between 1112 and 1128 there was a habitable dwelling at Grange, later occupied by the perpetual vicar of St. Giles, as vassal. The superiority of the land remained with the King.

During the fourteenth century the lands of Grange entered a period of uncertainty. In 1355 David II (1329–1370) withdrew the grants of lands made by David I, and in 1376 Robert II (1370–1390) gave the superiority of them to his son. In 1390 Robert III disponed his rights over the lands of Priestfield and Grange to one Andrew Wardlaw, whose exact identity remains doubtful as the charter has never been traced. However, it was James Wardlaw who resigned the lands back to James IV, and in 1506 the King granted them to John Cant, burgess of Edinburgh and his wife 'Agnes Carkettil'.

The Cants held sway at Grange from 1506 to 1631: although much is known of their fortunes, little has been traced of their fortune! Their ancestors, who included Adam Cant, Dean of Guild in 1450, had lived in the family house in Cant's Close, upon the gable end of which were the initials I.C.—A.K., Agnes' surname being spelt Kirkettil. John and Agnes had two sons, Thomas and Walter. Thomas, the heir, granted the lands of Grange in 1572 to his elder son John, and thence to Walter the younger, great grandson of John and Agnes. Walter the younger married Margaret Prestoun and after his death she married Alexander Thomson of Duddingston in 1594. A surviving lintel stone at Grange with the intriguing inscription REPOSE ALLEVRS ANNO 1592 prompted Mrs J. Stewart Smith to speculate as to its exact meaning:

Grange Loan looking west, 1900, with the entrance to St. Thomas Road on the left, and on the right, the entrance gates and lodge to Grange House. From the Yerbury Collection.

It is as though we had arrived at a distinctly marked epoch in the history of Sanctgeligrange, and a complete veil was suddenly cast over this hitherto notable family, whose old manor-place now mourned its master in silence.

The quaint inscription in Old French carved on the lintel of the original doorway, not only commemorates to us the exodus of the family, but also the transition of its possessors from the Romish to the Reformed faith. It is almost like a seal above the portal, closing it for a time.

That time was not long. Walter's son John married Katherine Creech in 1612 and another stone was placed above the 1592 inscription with the date 1613 and the initials I.C. and K.C. The unusual arrangement of the initials led MacGibbon

and Ross to conclude (incorrectly) that the names commemorated were KAY and CRICH or CREICH. The final
chapter for the Cants was in 1631 when John Cant agreed to
sell the estate to William Dick. The agreement was reached
during a round of golf on the Braid Hills after which the
contestants adjourned to Grange House to complete the
formalities.

THE DICKS AND THE LAUDERS

THE GRANGE'S GREATEST ERA began in 1631 with the arrival
of the Dick family, whose long period of tenure had some
anxious moments. William Dick had five sons and two
daughters: his heir was John who predeceased him by several
years. William was a man of very great wealth who had
acquired so much land (including the estate of Braid) that it
was said he could ride on his own estates all the way from
Linlithgow to North Berwick. As a staunch supporter of
King Charles he was an obvious choice for Lord Provost of
Edinburgh in 1638. His financial dealings, however, in
supporting both Charles I and the Covenanters eventually
brought appreciation from neither quarter. Hating Cromwell
even more than Episcopacy, he was induced to lend £20,000
to King Charles, a transaction which he later had cause to
regret. Had he confined his activities to Scotland he might
well have survived the financial and political storms around
him, but he lent large sums of money to England and the
loans were not recognised by the Commonwealth government. As a royalist he was fined by Oliver Cromwell and
faced imminent financial ruin. Despite going to London to
petition for return of the money advanced, he received very
little compensation. In 1655 he was seventy-five years of age,
and penniless. He died in the debtors' prison at Westminster
on 19th December 1655, escaping the ignominy of a pauper's
grave only by the intervention of Janet McMath, his daughter-
in-law. From her own private finances she paid for the body
to be returned to Edinburgh and buried at the north wall of
Greyfriars Churchyard. Unfortunately Dick's tomb was

After lending substantial sums of money to both Charles I and the Covenanters, William Dick of Grange House was confined to the debtors' prison in Westminster, where he died on 19th December 1655. From *The Grange of St. Giles.*

destroyed many years later when extensive alterations were made to the churchyard to accommodate a new north entrance.

On the death of Sir William Dick in 1655 his grandson, also William, eldest son of John Dick of Orkney, fell heir to the barony of Braid. His inheritance, however, was valueless as all that remained of the estate was substantial debt. Like his grandfather, he spent much of his time trying to recoup the family fortunes from the State, but without success. William was imprisoned and required constant support from his younger brother John. The young men's uncle, Sir Andrew Dick of Craig House, appointed himself to represent the family and succeeded in obtaining renewal of a small sum previously due from the State to Sir William's family. Although the sum of £5 per week was duly received, Sir Andrew appears to have retained it for his own use. Eventually William was released from prison by the intervention of Janet McMath who had financed the burial of the grandfather.

Janet McMath was widowed twice. Her only son William, second baron of Grange, inherited her estate in 1679 which passed to his son, also William, the third baron in 1695. The third baron, William Dick, married Dame Anne Seton and both were resident at Grange House during the eventful year of 1745. On his way to Holyrood, Prince Charles Edward Stuart visited Grange House where his hosts included Dame Anne's younger sisters Isabel and Jean Seton of Pitmedden. As a mark of respect the younger sister was chosen to present to the Prince a pure white rose from the House garden. In accepting it the Prince responded by taking a thistle from his bonnet and presented it to the elated young lady. Later the thistle was preserved in a small dome-shaped glass with the following inscription round the base:

> In 1745 Prince Charles honoured the House of Grange by visiting William Dick, its third Baron, and Anne Seton, his lady, and her sisters, Jane and Isabel. To mark the regard of his family from Queen Mary downwards for that of Seton, he took this thistle from his bonnet and presented it to the ladies. He afterwards received them at breakfast at Holyrood, and distinguished them at the Court.

The daughter of William Dick and Anne Seton was Isobel Dick who fell heir to the estate in 1755. Isobel's husband was

The tomb of Principal William Robertson of Edinburgh University, in Greyfriars Churchyard. Principal Robertson retired to Grange House but died shortly afterwards, in 1793. The taller tomb to the left is for William Adam, the architect. From *The Epitaphs and Monumental Inscriptions in Greyfriars Churchyard*.

Sir Andrew Lauder, 5th Baronet of Fountainhall. They had a son Andrew who took his mother's name of Dick but on the death of his father in 1769 he adopted the title Andrew Lauder-Dick, 6th Baronet of Fountainhall. Andrew preferred to live at Fountainhall and for several years Grange House was let to tenants. Some of the fields were let to Lord

Cockburn's father who lived at Hope Park on the north side of Sciennes Road, and Grange House was leased to John Forrest merchant burgess of Edinburgh. Perhaps the most eminent tenant, however, was Principal Robertson who moved to the Grange around 1792. William Robertson was born in 1721 the son of a parish minister at Borthwick in Midlothian. After studying at Edinburgh University he qualified as a minister and was appointed to Gladsmuir in 1753. He was also Moderator of the General Assembly in 1763. His connection with Edinburgh University spanned several decades: he was elected Principal in 1762 and was chosen to lay the foundation stone on 16th November 1789 of Robert Adam's new building for Edinburgh University in South Bridge. Among Robertson's major works were a *History of Scotland* in 1759 followed by a *History of Charles V* and a *History of America*. When Robertson came to Grange, however, he was already an old man and obviously less robust than he had been in former years. His quiet retreat served him for only a short time as he died at Grange House on 11th June 1793. He was buried in Greyfriars Churchyard in a huge mausoleum adjacent to that for William Adam the architect. In *Memorials of His Time* Lord Cockburn recalled the days when Principal Robertson visited his father's house at Hope Park:

> He was a very pleasant-looking old man; with an eye of great vivacity and intelligence, a large projecting chin, a small hearing trumpet fastened by a black ribbon to a button-hole in his coat, and a rather large wig powdered and curled. He struck us boys, even from the side-table, as being evidently fond of a good dinner; at which he sat, with his chin near his plate intent upon the real business of the occasion. This appearance, however, must have been produced by his deafness, because, when his eye told him there was something interesting, it was delightful to observe the animation with which he instantly applied his trumpet, when, having caught the scent, he followed it up, and was leader of the pack.

Sir Thomas Dick-Lauder, 7th Baronet of Fountainhall and 5th of Grange, who was responsible for feuing the Grange Estate during the mid-nineteenth century. From *The Grange of St. Giles*.

On the death of Andrew Lauder-Dick, 6th Baronet of Fountainhall, the estates passed to his son Thomas who reversed the hyphenated name and called himself Sir Thomas Dick-Lauder, 7th Baronet of Fountainhall and 5th of Grange. Sir Thomas was the member of the family most closely involved in the reconstruction of Grange House and the feuing of the estate for building purposes. He was born in 1784 and spent much of his early life out of Edinburgh, including a short time when he served in the Cameron Highlanders. His marriage to Charlotte Cumin, heiress to the estate of Relugas in Elginshire, produced a very large family of two sons and ten daughters. When he moved to the Grange in 1827 he had already established a reputation for literary achievement with *The Wolfe of Badenoch*, set in Morayshire. Other major works included the *Morayshire Floods* in 1830 and *Scottish Rivers*, published posthumously in 1874 from a series of essays written many years earlier. This latter work contains an account of the Jordan Burn in Edinburgh and also an illustration by Sir Thomas of Grange House before it was extended.

In the business and political world he showed equal talent, holding the position of Secretary to the Board of Trustees for Manufacturers, as well as being deeply involved, as a Liberal, with the passing of the Reform Bill in 1832. The 1832 Act increased the number of Scottish Members of Parliament from 45 to 53 and greatly extended the franchise. The political euphoria of the time was captured by Mrs J. Stewart Smith when she described one of the mass political rallies at which Sir Thomas presided. An open-air meeting at St. Ann's Yards to the east of Holyrood House was attended by 30,000 pro-Reform citizens who 'behaved with perfect obedience to the laws — no rioting, no indecorous language, the grave and silent masses [feeling] they were on the eve of a popular crisis'. After the Act was passed the Reform Jubilee in Edinburgh took place on Bruntsfield Links on 11th August when 40,000 onlookers watched a procession of 15,000 participants. The impromptu vocal tributes, steadily increasing

The tomb of Sir Thomas Dick-Lauder of Grange House on the east side of Grange Cemetery near Lovers' Loan. The five trefoiled panels commemorate several members of the Dick-Lauder and Cumin families. Photograph by Graham C. Cant.

in national pride, included *God Save the King, Rule Britannia* and *Scots Wha Hae.*

When Sir Thomas moved south to Edinburgh he engaged the famous architect W. H. Playfair to draw up plans for large-scale alterations and extensions to Grange House. In so doing he created a magnificent baronial home visited by many leading figures of the time, including Sir Walter Scott, Lord Cockburn of Bonaly, Lord Jeffrey of Craigcrook, Lord Rutherford of Lauriston, Dr John Brown and the artist minister from Duddingston, the Rev. John Thomson. Over dinner, or perhaps walking in the extensive grounds, the assembled company would no doubt vie with one another over their latest property developments at Bonaly Towers, Craigcrook Castle and Lauriston Castle.

As Sir Thomas continued to upgrade Grange House and its policies he realised the enormous potential in feuing out parts of his estate for building. Having secured an enabling Act of Parliament some years previously, he was able to see the first of the houses built in 1845. By that time Sir Thomas was sixty-one years of age and not in particularly good health. After a long illness his condition began to deteriorate, prompting Lord Cockburn to record in his diary on 19th March 1848:

> I saw Lauder on Sunday; he is obviously dying — but cheerful, gentle and kind — and making a slow, gradual death, of such pious gaiety and affectionate resignation that Philosophers and Christians might look on it and be instructed. Poor fellow, I wish I could hope. To me his disappearance will be like drawing a cold shade over life's sunniest scenery.

He died on 29th May 1848 at the age of sixty-three, mourned by a large family, his many friends, and the poor people of Edinburgh, to whom he had given generously. On the day of his burial the funeral cortège, consisting of a hearse preceded by ushers, the family carriage and twenty-two other carriages, left Grange House at 2.30 p.m. and drove via Grange Loan, Causewayside and Grange Road to Grange Cemetery.

Sir Thomas Dick-Lauder's grave, on the east side of the cemetery near Lovers' Loan, is marked by a broad tomb with a central pediment, below which are five trefoiled panels commemorating several members of the Dick-Lauder and Cumin families.

GRANGE HOUSE

THE EARLIEST DESCRIPTION OF GRANGE HOUSE is of 'a modest house with a jamb' situated on the Burgh Muir about two miles south of Edinburgh Castle. The earliest known illustration, believed to depict Grange House in 1700, is reproduced in the first volume of Storer's *Views in Edinburgh* published in 1820, under the chapter on the Hermitage of Braid. It is shown as a tall, L-shaped Scottish keep of three or four storeys with roof battlements and a single corbelled tower on the south-east corner above first-floor level. Abutting the east gable is a small lean-to slated outhouse which probably did not communicate directly with the main house. There is no way of knowing how much, if any, of Storer's view represents the original Grange House, but, judging from its appearance, it is at least as early as the sixteenth century. It is also interesting to note that Mrs J. Stewart Smith describes the Storer view 'with *two* turrets'. The copy illustration on page 5 of the *Grange of St. Giles* shows a slight variation in the detail of the dormer window, but neither Mrs J. Stewart Smith nor Storer gives any clear indication of where the second turret was. However, there is another illustration, dated 1825, drawn by Sir Thomas Dick-Lauder shortly before the Playfair extensions were started. Unlike the Storer view, which was taken from the south-east, Sir Thomas's drawing is done from the south-west. It shows a second turret starting from the first storey above ground level, within the re-entrant angle of the L-shape. There may be doubt, therefore, as to whether the second turret seen in Sir Thomas's 1825 drawing was extant in 1700.

Immediately before the Playfair extensions, Grange House consisted of a main rectangular block of three storeys plus an attic, running approximately east to west. A square stairtower projected from about the centre of the north wall, and a jamb or wing projected from the south wall in line with the east gable. A corbelled turret stair (the one not shown by Storer) was built in the re-entrant angle which opened to the south-west, but it did not start until the first floor. The entrance, with the famous lintel stone REPOSE ALLEVRS ANNO 1592, was in the west wall of the north stair tower, but the stair rose to the first floor only. Thereafter, access to the higher floors was by the turret stair in the angle facing the south-west. The space, which would have been taken by the north stairway above first-floor level, was utilised by a series of small chambers, one above the other, with access from the larger rooms on each floor. The basement floor of the main block was vaulted and the external masonry was of harled rubble with door and window dressings.

Some time between 1827 and 1831 Grange House was transformed into a much grander and more comfortable baronial residence by the additions designed by W. H. Playfair. These extensions more than doubled the available accommodation and were so skilfully integrated with the original house that even MacGibbon & Ross commented 'that at first sight one hardly knows where the old work ends and the new begins'. The additions were built to the east and south of the existing building, incorporating a new entrance on the north-east corner. Semi-octagonal towers were constructed on the north-west and south-west corners of the original house; extensive balconies were added with commanding views to the south; and the steeply pitched roof was punctuated with pedimented dormer windows.

Internally the arrangement of the rooms was altered to suit the new accommodation. The new entrance gave access through an inner entrance hall to a wide staircase with an oak balustrade. Above the portal were the sculptured arms of the Dick-Lauder and Cumin families and the date of reconstruction, 1827. The ground floor contained the kitchen and servants' quarters whilst the first floor was given over to the principal rooms. A new dining room, measuring forty-five feet by eighteen, was formed out of the dining room and drawing room of the old house. The walls and part of the ceiling were of oak panelling, ornamented by carved heads of monks and abbots. A new T-shaped drawing room, designed by Playfair, was lit by a large oriel window to the south and a balcony leading to the garden on the west. The new drawing room was also in oak, in keeping with the remainder of the house. An extensive library, in which Sir Thomas worked on his many literary projects lay between the dining room and the drawing room, in what was the jamb or wing of the original keep. The upper floors contained Sir Thomas's bedroom, Lady Dick-Lauder's boudoir, and a series of descriptive apartments — the Pink Room, the Green Room, the Daisy Room, the Lilac Room and the Day Nursery.

The earliest known illustration of Grange House, in 1700, shows a tall L-shaped Scottish keep with roof battlements and a single corbelled tower on the south-east corner. From Storer's *Views of Edinburgh*.

Unfortunately the Victorian writers, who described Grange House in such a pleasing and romantic style, held back from commenting on such 'vulgarities' as the stables, the vegetable garden, the water supply, the drainage system and above all the toilets and the disposal of sewage.

The garden contained several unusual features, some more conspicuous than others. Much of the five or six acres of ground was laid out in ornamental lawns with walks and terraces on different levels, reached by flights of steps with heavy balustrades. Close to the bowling green were four female statues facing north, south, east and west. These were presented to the family by Alexander Mitchell Innes of Ayton Castle on his marriage to one of the daughters, Charlotte: 'I have taken one maiden and left you four!' remarked the young groom as he made off with the animated one.

Within a few yards of the bowling green lay the dogs' cemetery — and the dogs, who had earned themselves a place in history, either by heroic deed or constant companionship. For Brontë the epitaph competes in length with many in Grange Cemetery nearby:

> From Newfoundland his high-bred fathers came,
> Lord of the sea-Brontë his gallant name —
> To reasoning man ensample he not be,
> For who so free from vice and sin as he?
> Urged by his generous heart, a young to save
> He dived — and dragged him from the whelming wave —
> But all, alas! too late — No life remained; —
> The noble dog: then be not too severe
> If o'er this turf where Brontë lies we drop a tear.

5.7.1838

In a quiet and overgrown corner of the garden was the Monk's Seat, a solid stone structure which attracted all manner of romantic stories. Given the ecclesiastical associations with Grange House, it would be tempting to imagine that this seat was used by the monks and abbots of yesteryear. This supposition is greatly reinforced by two inscriptions on the seat: on the lower section is the old Scottish proverb — HE YT THOLIS OVERCVMMIS; and along the back in a different style of lettering are the words: IN THE IS AL MY TRAIST 1569. The secular Cants were in residence at Grange House sixty-three years prior to 1569 but in any case there is a more practical explanation, alluded to by Wilson in *Memorials of Edinburgh in the Olden Time*. The year 1569 was also the date of construction of Robert Gourlay's house in Old Bank Close. When the house was being demolished in 1824 a decision was taken to save the lintel stone which happened to say: O LORD IN THE IS AL MY TRAIST

1569. As the demolition men began to remove the lintel it was discovered that the words O LORD became detached from the remainder of the inscription. On closer examination (and perhaps stifling an obvious blasphemy) the workmen found that the detached words were carved in oak and made to match the rest. The remaining words, in stone, were eventually brought to Grange House and incorporated in what became known as the Monk's Seat. An illustration of the seat appears in *The Grange of St. Giles*. The actual lintel stone carries only the words IN THE IS AL MY, and TRAIST 1569 appears to be on a separate stone partly hidden by foliage. It is likely, therefore, that at some time in the past a similar stone carried the missing words at the beginning of the inscription. It is not known how or when the mason came to sever his connection with O LORD.

When *The Grange of St. Giles* was written in 1897 Grange House had ceased to be the baronial home of the Dick-Lauder family. From at least the mid-1870s it had been let to the Misses Mouat for use as a ladies' college, which had previously operated from No. 9 South Gray Street. During the early years of the twentieth century the fabric of the building began to show signs of lack of maintenance, caused by long periods when it was empty. By 1936 the whole structure was in such a poor state of repair that it was beyond restoration. Almost eight hundred years of history, encapsulated in a huge pile of decaying masonry, surrounded by several acres of prime residential land, fell victim to the only practical solution — housing. Letters of protest poured into the Edinburgh press, but to no avail. The house was too large for any one family and no commercial or educational use could be found in view of the high cost of renovation and subsequent upkeep. The demolition men moved in, salvaging at least the ancient sculptured stones and the Monk's Seat, which were removed to Huntly House Museum for safe keeping. On 19th November 1936 a photograph in the *Evening Dispatch* showed the house in the final throes of extinction: all the 1827 Playfair extensions had gone; the upper storeys of the original square keep were still standing along with most of the south jamb. This tragic roofless stump bore a striking resemblance to Storer's view of 1700. It was as if the original keep had gradually become ruinous over the preceding centuries, without ever having been visited by the architectural flair of Playfair. Local interest intensified as the estate grounds were laid open to the public gaze. Its long history was recalled and numerous predictions were made as to what would be found when the most ancient parts of the building eventually succumbed. All were without foundation, except the prediction of one elderly lady (the 'Brahan Seer' of Grange) who warned the workmen to be on their guard for a deep well hidden in the grounds. Although the story was told with a hint of the supernatural, the existence of a well would be commonplace, even if its location was uncertain. However, early in September 1936 a well was found by workmen excavating for a new boundary wall on the east side of the estate. It was about thirty-seven feet deep, seven feet of which were filled with clear spring water. The shaft was fitted with an ancient wooden draw-pipe formed from a hollowed-out tree trunk with an iron plunger down through the centre. Some distance down the shaft a small recess could be seen, which was imaginatively assumed to be the exit point of an escape tunnel from Grange House. Such a tunnel may well have been built, either as a means of escape or as a place of safety for deeds and valuables, but it does not seem very likely that it would emerge halfway down a deep well with a sudden drop into several feet of water. The notion that the recess was a secret tunnel was quickly abandoned and the shaft was filled with concrete. There have been several other references to a secret passageway, the most ambitious of which is said to have extended from Grange House to the Old Town of Edinburgh. However romantic the tradition might be, the distance involved and the difficulty of negotiating the Burgh Loch suggest that such a tunnel never existed.

Ghosts are different: they are neither proved, nor disproved, by either common sense or a knowledge of civil

One of the Wyvern Pillars which once formed an old gateway within the grounds of Grange House, repositioned at the south end of Lovers' Loan when Grange House was demolished in 1936. The other pillar is also on Grange Loan a few hundred yards to the east. Photograph by Phyllis M. Cant.

engineering. Over the years, Grange House has recorded several ghosts, in different guises. The green lady was widely rumoured to exist, but never sighted in any authentic account. Doubt was also cast on the haunted tower but a mirror, with unusual properties, seems to have been in a different mould. Its ability to reflect ghostly apparitions, other than the person standing in front of it, won some acclaim in an advertisement which appeared in the *Edinburgh Evening News* on 30th May 1936. Under the heading 'Mystic Mirror of Grange' the sum of £26 was asked by Dowells Ltd. of Edinburgh for an 'old Venetian mirror 7 ft. by 4 ft. 2 in., known as the Mystic Mirror of Grange House, Edinburgh, accredited to have reflected images of persons not present'.

The traditional ghost of Grange House, however, is the miser who, from time to time, rolled a barrel of gold coins through the oldest part of the house. It was said that if he were sighted by any member of the family they would instantly inherit the fortune. Miss Cornelia Dick-Lauder felt compelled to believe the story after hearing an account of it from a young female visitor to the house, who had not previously known of the ghost. Whilst sleeping in Lady Lauder's boudoir the visitor was suddenly awakened by hearing a rumbling sound as if something was being rolled along the corridor. The noise increased as it approached her room and stopped exactly opposite her door. The sounds recurred on a second and third occasion, accompanied by the sound of heavy footsteps. Although the visitor was petrified, it does not appear that she summoned attention from other persons in the house, and in the morning she left without mentioning the incident. Later she told her sister. Shortly after the incident, whilst the same visitor and her sister were having a meal at Grange House, an inquisitive diner asked Sir Thomas if the house was haunted. In reply the story was related of the old miser who rolled a barrel of gold coins about the house, whereupon the one sister looked at the other sister, who looked as though she would faint. The visitor retold her story, but as no member of the family ever saw the old miser, the fortune was never claimed.

Perhaps the most compelling story is that related by Mrs J. Stewart Smith in her Introduction to *The Grange of St. Giles.* In a letter to Miss Cornelia Dick-Lauder of Lauder House the author explains what inspired her to write such a comprehensive history of Grange House. The seed of discovery lay in a curious 'dream-vision' experienced by the author after a visit to Grange House. At the time of the visit Mrs Stewart Smith points out that she knew nothing of the history of Grange House, nor anything of its various occupants. She says that 'a series of tableaux presented themselves before me' on 26th January 1891, which appeared to be the re-enactment of important historical events. The detailed notes taken at the time eventually took on a significant meaning as Mrs Stewart Smith's research confirmed the true historical basis of her uncanny glimpse into the family history.

The remaining parts of Grange House appear to have been demolished by early 1938, when Canon Thomas Hannan reported that the 'old avenue from the Loan is being filled up to the level of the adjoining soil and the great trees have been cut down — the north and centre part of the house have been demolished'. The arched doorway and lodge house on the north side of Grange Loan were removed as new houses began to appear in Grange Loan and Grange Crescent. The rusticated gate pillars, supporting the 'Lauder Griffins', from an earlier entrance to the house, were saved and rebuilt on the east and west extremities of the Grange House policies. These heraldic beasts have, perhaps understandably, been referred to by many writers as griffins, as the mythical griffin appears in the coat of arms of the Lauder family. As a result of recent research, first published in *The Grange — A Case for Conservation,* the better opinion is that the rusticated pillars are topped, not with griffins, but with wyverns. Griffins had the forepart of an eagle with beaks, wings and forelegs bearing claws, and the hindquarters of a lion: wyverns had the head of a dragon issuing fire, wings and the barbed tail of a serpent. Although the Grange Loan beasts have suffered damage to detail over the years they are clearly wyverns.

In the chapter 'The Living Past' in Volume 2 of *Historic South Edinburgh* Charles J. Smith recalls his discussion with Sir George Dick-Lauder, 12th Baronet of Fountainhall and Grange. Although Grange House has been demolished for more than fifty years, all the priceless heirlooms and portraits are still in the possession of the Dick-Lauder family. Many interesting photographs of Grange House are also held with a host of private papers yet to be catalogued.

Although not strictly part of Grange House, the Penny Well at the east end of Grange Loan has from time immemorial been associated with the old manor house of Grange. Its age is uncertain. Tradition suggests that it dates from the early sixteenth century when the Convent of Sienna was established at Sciennes. The earliest recorded date, however, is 1716 when the Penny Well was used to denote the position of three acres of land being sold by William Johnstone of Westerhall to William Dick of Grange. The origin of the name is also in doubt. In the middle of the nineteenth century it is said that an elderly widow living nearby sold the water at one penny a cup. Unfortunately the theory is defeated by the 1716 land reference and, in any case, a penny for a glass of water in 1716 was probably higher than the price of the best ale.

Around 1870 the well dried up, possibly due to interference with the water table during construction of houses nearby. In an effort to improve the intermittent supply of water a deep pit was dug in an adjacent garden in which the water was collecting. In the course of the excavation a large block of hard sandstone was found measuring thirty-two inches square, in the centre of which was a circular basin with a diameter of twenty-eight inches and a depth of ten and a half inches. At the time of discovery it was believed to be an ancient baptismal font.

The Penny Well has been repaired on numerous occasions in the twentieth century but water has not flowed in it for many years. All that remains is the vertical flat stone outline, without fittings, and the inscription PENNY WELL.

CHAPTER 3

THE
EARLY HISTORY
OF SCIENNES

THE EARLY HISTORY OF SCIENNES is dominated by the foundation of two religious houses, within a few hundred yards of one another, at the east end of what is now Sciennes Road. The first to be established was the Chapel of St. John the Baptist, followed about five years later by the Convent of Saint Catherine of Sienna. No buildings survive from that period but the foundation, and eventual demise, of the Chapel and the Convent are reasonably well documented, and it is possible, even today, to trace the areas of ground on which they were built. Considerable additional information has also been made available from the lengthy legal battles which raged between the Town and various local landowners in the mid-eighteenth century.

At the west end of Sciennes Road the hamlets of Westerhall and New Campbeltown were in existence long before Marchmont was built on the estate of Sir George Warrender of Bruntisfield House. The eventual destruction of these communities was discussed at length in *Marchmont in Edinburgh* but is included in Chapter 4 where relevant to the development of Sciennes in the nineteenth century.

CHAPEL OF ST. JOHN:
CONVENT OF SIENNA

THE RECORDED HISTORY OF SCIENNES dates from at least the

beginning of the sixteenth century when the district formed part of the ancient Burgh Muir. Its position, well outside the protection of Edinburgh's city wall, did not, however, deter Sir John Crawfurd, canon of St. Giles, in his bid to erect a chapel at Sciennes 'for the benefit of the souls of the founder, his kindred, the reigning monarch and the Magistrates of Edinburgh'. In 1511 Sir John obtained the feu of four and a half acres of land to the west of Causewayside, approximately L-shaped, stretching northwards from Sciennes House Place to the north side of Sciennes Place, and then westwards to where it joined the messuage of the Grange of St. Giles. Sciennes Place was not, of course, built until many years after 1511, but the north boundary of Sir John's land was the hamlet of Mureburgh, later occupied by the tenement buildings of Sciennes Place, Sciennes and Lord Russell Place. To this extensive piece of ground he annexed a further eighteen acres feued from John Cant some time between 1506 and 1513. This latter acquisition lay to the north-east corner of the Grange of St. Giles, and, therefore, conveniently abutted the south-western portion of the four and a half acres to the east. The combined twenty-two and a half acres became the scene, albeit for a relatively short period, of one of the most interesting chapters in the religious life of Edinburgh in the sixteenth century.

In February 1512, following completion of the Chapel dedicated to St. John the Baptist and St. John the Evangelist, a formal charter was drawn up conveying the full acreage for the support of the chaplain, and defining his duties at considerable length:

> [He] shall be a secular chaplain and priest, bound by no religious vow, of laudable report, and honest conversation; and he shall be held bound every day, when he shall be ready at the high altar, to celebrate Mass in the said church and in this manner, viz: every Monday a Mass of Requiem, and every Friday, of the Five Wounds of our Lord, Jesus Christ, unless he shall be hindered lawfully by some greater double feast.

Even if the demanding ecclesiastical timetable had allowed occasional moments of respite, the charter was equally direct in its condemnation of the most likely forms of distraction:

> Nor shall it be lawful for the said chaplain to have or keep a loose woman or concubine in his chamber or house, nor to play cards, nor be a common gamester or engage in similar games of chance . . .

William Moir Bryce, writing in the *Book of the Old Edinburgh Club* in 1918, observed that Sir John added a very picturesque touch by the appointment of a hermit to assist at the chapel. The applicant was required to be a man of 'advanced age, of good life and sound constitution' to reside permanently at the chapel and to wear a white robe, having on his breast the picture of the head of St. John the Baptist. His duties included the saying of prayers, assisting the chaplain, and cleaning and purifying the chapel buildings, in return for which he was given the use of a house and an acre of ground near the southern boundary of the chapel grounds. Having established this basic lifestyle, the chaplain and his hermit might well have remained in comparative solitude for many years had it not been for 'a rival bid', promulgated by a small band of devout females of high rank, who also wished to establish a religious order at Sciennes.

The Convent of St. Catherine of Sienna of the Dominican Order was founded by Lady Janet Seton whose husband George, third Lord Seton, was killed at the Battle of Flodden, 1513, along with many other Scottish nobles. Having been widowed at a comparatively early age, Lady Janet decided, with others, to devote the rest of her life to the service of God. She came to Sciennes and with the assistance of Elizabeth Auchinleck, daughter of James Auchinleck, and the Lady of the Bass (probably Agnes Fairlaw, wife of Sir Robert Lauder of the Bass), began the task of establishing a new religious house for ladies in Scotland. Progress was

Remains of the Convent of St. Catherine of Sienna founded by Lady Janet Seton in 1518, extensively damaged in 1544 by the Earl of Hertford, and destroyed in 1567. Parts of the convent building survived as late as 1871. From *The Convent of Saint Catherine of Sienna*.

remarkably swift: in 1516 land on which to erect the convent building was acquired from Sir John Crawfurd, who also handed over the use of his chapel built only a few years earlier. On 29th January 1517 Papal authority was received under a Bull of Pope Leo X, and in 1518 the convent was completed, the first prioress being Josina Henryson. Although Sir John appears to have been content to transfer the chapel as a gift to the sisters, he did stipulate that it was to be returned to him in the event of their ceasing to use it for the purpose intended.

The convent was built on the south side of Sciennes Road, near its east end on land now occupied by the north end of St. Catherine's Place. Although no original plans or drawings survive, a fairly accurate description of the basic layout can be gleaned from various sources. The buildings were unpretentious with few ornamentations, probably of one storey, surrounded by a high stone wall, part of which abutted onto Sciennes Road. There was one entrance only, on the east side, which led through open garden ground to the old Chapel of St. John. A deep well provided a good supply of fresh water and a small burn was used for sanitary and drainage purposes, but there were few other comforts. The area of ground within the walls was 1 acre 3 roods 2 ells with a further 17 falls 2½ ells outside, giving a total area of 1 acre 3 roods 17 falls and 4½ ells, or nearly two acres. Within this small compact area the sisters established a solitary, but workable, lifestyle for several years without significant dependence on the outside world.

It did not, however, remain like that for long, its eventual decline and destruction being closely linked to the political and religious upheavals which lay ahead. The sisters' conventual lifestyle was harshly interrupted in 1544 during the Earl of Hertford's invasion of Edinburgh, when the convent was attacked along with the nearby houses of Grange, Whitehouse and Bruntisfield. William Moir Bryce advances cogent arguments for the belief that despite this obvious setback the convent survived and was again in operation in 1555, although not on such a large scale. By 1565 the number of sisters was eighteen, whereas the original Bull of 1517 had allowed for up to thirty. Two years later, the convent was completely destroyed in the religious fervour which accompanied the Reformation in 1567. Lady Jane Seton, who founded the convent in 1516, survived the Hertford invasion by several years but died at Sciennes in 1558 after forty-three years' service, a decade before its eventual demise.

After the convent community was dispersed in 1567 the last prioress, Dame Christian Ballenden, feued the lands to Henry Kincaid, second son of John Kincaid of Warriston. It is uncertain how long the lands were in the possession of the Kincaids but by the middle of the seventeenth century the estate had passed to Janet McMath, wife of William Dick of

Sarum Breviary published at Rouen in 1496, bequeathed to Edinburgh Town Council in 1580 by Clement Litill. Courtesy of Edinburgh University Library.

Grange. Their son, also William, became heir in 1679 to various lands 'including 18 arable acres of the Sheines, of old termed Sanct Geile-Grange, with the garden of Sheines'. When William Dick died in 1755, without male issue, the estate of Sciennes passed to his daughter who married Sir Andrew Lauder of Fountainhall.

Perhaps one of the most compelling and authoritative

accounts of the history of the convent is contained in *The Convent of Saint Catherine of Sienna* by George Seton, Advocate, who was writing at a time when the last vestiges of the convent building were under threat from residential development. His account was originally contained in a paper read before the Architectural Institute of Scotland on 11th April 1867 but was later expanded and printed for private circulation in 1871. Whilst most modern writers have relied heavily upon his research into the early history of the convent, it is perhaps his personal observation of its final demise which is so compelling. In the paper delivered to the Institute in 1867 Seton tells his audience that the small remaining fragment of the convent will probably 'be entirely extinguished at no very distant date, to make way for the suburban abode of some Edinburgh shopkeeper'. By 1871 his worst fears were confirmed in a footnote to the printed edition:

> In little more than four years, this prediction has been at least partially fulfilled. During the summer of 1871, the fragment in question was razed to the ground, and its site is now occupied by a semi-detached villa erected by his congregation for a Wesleyan Methodist minister. With that gentleman's permission, I propose to affix a cast-iron tablet on the corner of the villa, with a short inscription indicative of the site of the Convent . . .

The house is No. 16 St. Catherine's Place where the plaque still exists, although not on the corner of the villa.

Nothing remains of the convent now. The names Sciennes, Sienna and St. Catherine are commemorated in street names nearby, and there is no doubt as to the area of ground on which the convent and garden stood, i.e. stretching along the south side of Sciennes Road from St. Catherine's Pace to Sciennes House Place. The Chapel of St. John is believed to have stood on the approximate site of Sciennes Hill House in

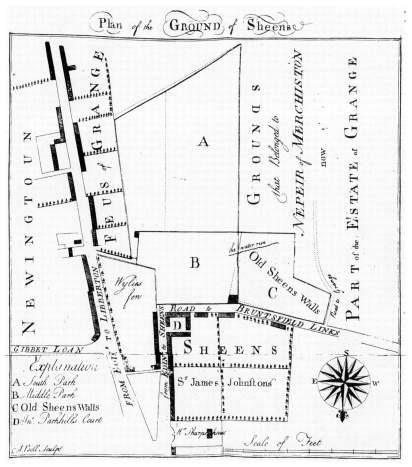

Map of the Sciennes area produced for the eighteenth-century law case between the Dick-Lauder family and Sir James Johnstone of Westerhall, Session Papers, vol. 90: 5, 1764. Courtesy of the Signet Library, Parliament Square, Edinburgh.

Sciennes House Place, details of which are given later in this chapter. Wilson in *Memorials of Edinburgh in the Olden Time* suggests that stones from the ruined chapel form part of the garden wall of Sciennes Hill House but these are not now identifiable. There are several references to the chapel and the convent in the Burgh Records conveniently brought together in a series first edited by the Scottish Burgh Records Society. Perhaps the most interesting documentary evidence, however, is held in Edinburgh University Library, being a printed copy of a Breviary presented by Sir John Crawfurd to the chapel on its completion. This important document was bequeathed to Edinburgh Town Council in 1580 on the death of Clement Litill, along with his entire collection of books, which became the nucleus of the University Library in 1583. Further details of the collection are enumerated in *Clement Litill and His Library* by Charles P. Finlayson, published in 1980.

DICK-LAUDER OF GRANGE
V
JOHNSTONE OF WESTERHALL

ALTHOUGH THE CONVENT ceased to exist after the Reformation the remains of it were described in some detail, along with the surrounding district of Sciennes, in a lengthy legal battle between two wealthy landowners in the middle of the eighteenth century. The argument, eventually resolved in favour of Dick-Lauder, was reported in papers running to several hundred pages, preserved in the Signet Library in Parliament Square, under the reference Session Papers vol. 90:5, 1764. It concerned the area of ground known as Sheens Walls, within which the convent had stood. The case began as early as February 1760 when the Lauder family brought an action against the Lord Provost and Magistrates of Edinburgh, and against Hary Guthrie, Writer in Edinburgh:

> concluding that they should remove from the old yard, orchard and place of Sheens with the houses and biggings now waste and ruinous being the ground within old Sheens walls, originally set in tack as the pursuers averred to the said good town for the yearly rent of 40 merks Scots, and continued in their

possession by tacit relocation; and of late possessed by the deceased Mr Alexander Bayne, advocate, professor of the Scots law in the university of Edinburgh, who enclosed the same with a stone and lime dike built out of the ruins of the said old walls of the Monastery of the Sheens, and thereafter possessed by his heirs and now by the said Hary Guthrie, Writer in Edinburgh.

Sir James Johnstone's involvement arose from his having obtained a feu of the lands in question from the town in 1731, which he sub-feued to Alexander Bayne in 1735. The question, therefore, was whether the disputed land, Sheens Walls, belonged to Dick-Lauder or to the town, with subsequent legal title to Johnstone and Bayne. In considering the evidence, the court looked, firstly, at the various charters and then heard oral evidence from several witnesses on the nature and extent of the ground known as Sheens Walls. Confusion arose between two separate, but similar, pieces of ground, both of which were surrounded by high stone walls. Dick-Lauder's productions showed that he had a right to part of the 'yards of Sheens' and the town also laid claim to a similar piece of ground. It was alleged that in 1602 the town had taken possession of the disputed piece of ground 'for the conveniency of the persons infected with the plague', for which the town had paid forty merks damages for that year. Incredibly, there was also evidence to suggest that after the plague Dick-Lauder's predecessor (Herbert) had recovered possession of the disputed land, but that owing to an administrative error the town had continued paying damages of forty merks per annum for one hundred and sixty years. In court, the town's stance appears to have been that if Dick-Lauder could identify clearly the boundaries of his ground he could retain it, but, if not, he would need to content himself with forty merks annually, notwithstanding that the town still maintained that the original piece of ground had been restored to the owner after the plague. In the course of the argument even the description *Sheens Walls* was called into question when counsel maintained:

> That the appellation of the Sheens Walls is not a legal designation of any particular place . . . but is an appellation which has crept in from custom, and has been given to this inclosure, either because it was surrounded with very high walls or because it was full of ruins which generally among the vulgar go by the name of *walls*, and in particular this name is very commonly given in different parts of the country to ruins of religious houses.

In addition to the niceties of the legal arguments the case is of great interest to local historians for the secondary details concerning the general locality of Sciennes and the names and occupations of the various witnesses. Their evidence related mainly to the dispute which arose as to whether the old convent lay to the south of Sciennes Road or to the north of Sciennes Road at its junction with Sciennes (marked D on the Plan of the Ground of Sheens). Three witnesses said it lay to the north. The first was James Mitchell, employed as a wright at Causewayside, who maintained that:

> [The] inclosure is known by the name of the old Sheens walls, or an old Popish chapel, or something of that nature. On the north side of the Sheens loaning [Sciennes Road] where John Parkhill's house now stands there was an old house of about three storeys and garrets high, very strong built with old fashioned windows which was called the monastery-house.

Mitchell's evidence was confirmed by a stonemason, Thomas Hutchison, who agreed that before Parkhill's house was built the site had been occupied by a very old house called the manse or the monastery, which he had been employed to

opposite

Sciennes Hill House, built c. 1741, the only recorded meeting place of Robert Burns and Sir Walter Scott, when it was the home of Adam Ferguson, Professor of Moral Philosophy at Edinburgh University. The date of the drawing and the identity of the artist are unknown. Courtesy of the National Gallery of Scotland, Prints and Drawings Department.

demolish. His recollection, under oath, was 'that the house was very strongly built and ill to take down'. Unfortunately for counsel, the evidence of these two seemingly good witnesses was seriously weakened by the third witness, John Hill of Grange Loan. Although Hill agreed that the convent or monastery was on the north, it was clear that his understanding of a monastery was 'a very old strong-built house with small windows'. Opposing counsel was not slow to exploit the weakness, in customary sardonic tone: 'it is plain that the witness last quoted would call every old house with small windows a monastery'.

Three witnesses were also called to show that the convent was on the south side of Sciennes Road. Their evidence was altogether more compelling, especially that from Thomas Hope of Rankeillor, then aged eighty-three, who recalled that he had seen the old ruins of the convent within the piece of ground on the south side of Sciennes Loaning, and that they were reckoned to be the ruins of the monastery. Furthermore he was able to weaken the 'north' argument by recalling the old house on Parkhill's site and saying that he had never heard of it being called the monastery house. Sir Thomas was backed by two other witnesses, both of whom were masons, who had been employed to use the old stones of Sheens Walls to build retaining dykes in 1735 for Alexander Bayne who had sub-feued the ground from Sir James Johnstone. One of the masons, James Archibald, recalled that when he was taking stones from the ruin, an old gentleman passed by and told him that it was the ruins of the monastery and pointed out a particular part of it called the vestry where the priest had put on his robes.

After reviewing the case in *The Convent of Saint Catherine of Sienna* George Seton, Advocate, noted at the close of this very lengthy legal dispute in 1766 that although Dick-Lauder won the day he gained only £5: 15s: 6d. per annum against legal expenses of more than £200 'or forty eight years purchase of all that he gets by the decision in his favour'.

The Plan of the Ground of Sheens prepared for the case of Dick-Lauder v Johnstone is of particular interest when studied in conjunction with the information given by the witnesses. In the interpretation of the map, however, care must be taken to remember that its primary use was the legal process, and therefore some buildings, though prominent, might have been omitted had they not been considered relevant to the case. Even with this reservation the basic layout is instantly recognisable. Four main streets are shown. Present-day Causewayside is shown as 'From Edinburgh to Libberton' with Gibbet Loan off to the east on the site of what is now East Preston Street. Sciennes Road is shown as 'Road to Bruntsfield Links' and Sciennes is described as 'From Edinburgh to Sheens'. Old Sheens Walls (the site of the Convent of St. Catherine of Sienna) is shown clearly to the south of Sciennes Road, with a small road or track leading southwards to Grange House and Grange Farm. There is no sign of Sciennes House Place (formerly Braid Place), Sciennes Hill Place or Sciennes Gardens. Wylie's Feu has the approximate boundaries of the land first obtained by Sir John Crawfurd when he founded the Chapel of St. John more than two centuries earlier. The only buildings shown on the feu are a line of cottages on its west side, facing onto the road from Edinburgh to Sheens. The square parcel of land called Sheens (with Sir James' surname spelt differently to that in the law report) is neatly divided into quarters by lines of trees, and Parkhill's Court is shown on the extreme south-east corner. The site of Parkhill's Court previously known as Scheyns Place was of great antiquity even in the middle of the eighteenth century. Sir William Johnstone lived there from 1720 to 1730 in the very old house 'with iron staunchels in the windows', mistaken in the court case for the convent or monastery. It was two storeys in height forming part of a square or courtyard in which there was a deep well. An old malt kiln stood at the east end of the house adjacent to an open barn.

The site was latterly occupied by the registered office of Bertrams Ltd, the famous manufacturers of paper-making machinery. When the firm closed and the building was demolished in 1987 the ground was redeveloped for modern brick-built flats retaining the historic name Sienna. During preparation of the site the eighteenth century well was located, and capped.

SCIENNES HILL HOUSE

SCIENNES HILL HOUSE was built around 1741 as a substantial three-storey detached house in a large garden reached by a driveway which ran due south from entrance gates in the small lane now known as Sciennes Place. The principal doorway on the north façade was reached by an imposing flight of steps giving access to a house of considerable architectural refinement in its main staircase, cornices and wainscoting. At one time, a side gate, facing Sciennes Road, contained a date panel, 1741, with three plain shields under a moulding, but unfortunately they did not contain any details of the original owner. The side gate was demolished in the 1860s when the tenement buildings of Braid Place (now Sciennes House Place) were being constructed.

Whilst the house is of interest on account of its age, there can be no doubt that its place in history was secured in the winter of 1786~87 during its occupation by Adam Ferguson, Professor of Moral Philosophy at Edinburgh University. At one of Ferguson's literary evenings, the exact date of which is not known, Scotland's two greatest literary giants, Burns and Scott, met for the first and only recorded occasion. Burns, visiting Edinburgh at the height of his literary popularity, made a lasting impression on Scott, who recalled the event several years later in a letter to his son-in-law, and biographer, J. G. Lockhart:

> I was a lad of fifteen in 1786~7, when he came first to Edinburgh, but had sense and feeling enough to be much interested in his poetry, and would have given

The bronze plaque on Sciennes Hill House in Sciennes House Place commemorating the meeting there of Robert Burns and Sir Walter Scott in the winter of 1786-87. Photograph by Phyllis M. Cant.

the world to know him; but I had very little acquaintance with any literary people, and still less with the gentry of the west country, the two sets that he most frequented. Mr Thomas Grierson was at that time a clerk of my father's. He knew Burns, and promised to ask him to his lodgings to dinner, but had no opportunity to keep his word, otherwise, I might have seen more of this distinguished man. As it was, I saw him one day at the late venerable Professor Ferguson's, where there were several gentlemen of literary reputation, among whom I remember the celebrated Mr Dugald Stewart. Of course we youngsters sat silent, looked and listened. The only thing I remember which was remarkable in Burns' manner, was the effect produced upon him by a print of Bunbury's, representing a soldier lying dead on the snow, his dog sitting in misery on the one side, on the other his widow, with a child in her arms. These lines were written beneath: —

'Cold on Canadian hills, or Minden's plain,
Perhaps that parent wept her soldier slain;
Bent o'er her babe, her eyes dissolved in dew,
The big drops, mingling with the milk he drew,
Gave the sad presage of his future years,
The child of misery baptized in tears.'

Burns seemed much affected by the print, or rather the ideas which it suggested to his mind. He actually shed tears. He asked whose the lines were, and it chanced that nobody but myself remembered that they occur in a half forgotten poem of Langhorne's called by the unpromising title of 'The Justice of the Peace'. I whispered my information to a friend present, who mentioned it to Burns, who rewarded me with a look and a word, which, though of mere civility, I then received, and still recollect, with very great pleasure.

The evening was, no doubt, a memorable one for Scott, and perhaps many other budding literati, but for some reason the exact date of it is not now recorded. Although Sciennes Hill House was accepted for many years as the meeting place of Burns and Scott, as recently as 1926 a minor controversy arose as to whether this was accurate. On 19th March 1926 James Milligan, President of the Edinburgh Sir Walter Scott Club, wrote to William Cowan at No. 47 Braid Avenue asking if the Edinburgh Burns Club was willing to join with the Edinburgh Sir Walter Scott Club in placing a tablet on Sciennes Hill House to commemorate the meeting between Burns and Scott in 1787. Milligan advanced the opinion, which he had heard from another source, that in 1787 Professor Ferguson was living in Argyle Square and not Sciennes Hill House, as generally believed. In the ensuing correspondence it was obvious that the information given in city directories was inconclusive, requiring further research at Register House. This revealed that the disposition for the sale of Ferguson's house in Argyle Square was dated 3rd October 1786 and that for the purchase of Sciennes Hill House was dated 11th October 1786. This lengthy and detailed research, on a point of considerable importance, was the subject of an article by James Milligan in *Chambers's Journal* for November 1926 in which he puts all doubt to rest: 'This, we venture to suggest is positive proof that Professor Ferguson was living in Sciennes Hill House during the period of Burns' visit to Edinburgh from 28th November 1786 to 6th May 1787, and that the meeting between Scott and Burns took place there'.

As a result of the research a bronze tablet was erected on the north elevation of the house at the instigation of the Edinburgh District Burns Clubs Association and the Edinburgh Sir Walter Scott Club. It bears the following inscription:

THIS TABLET COMMEMORATES
THE MEETING
OF ROBERT BURNS AND
SIR WALTER SCOTT
WHICH TOOK PLACE HERE
IN THE WINTER OF 1786-87

The meeting of Burns and Scott at Sciennes Hill House is also the subject of a painting by Charles Martin Hardie A.R.S.A., whose studio was, for a time, in Dean village.

At the present day, the house, devoid of most of its architectural features, forms part of a row of tenement buildings on the north side of Sciennes House Place. At first glance it is not obviously different to the buildings on either side of it, but closer examination reveals significant differences in the stonework. The front of the tenement of No. 5 is actually the rear elevation of the original house, the more ornate frontage being visible only from the back green area entered through the stairway of No. 7. The building is three storeys in height with attic windows in the roof space. The elevation to Sciennes House Place is of random rubble

51

incorporating single arched stones across many of the windows, and an unusual string course between the first and second storeys. The front (viewed from the back green area) is very much more ornate, with faced stonework, door and window embellishments. In 1988 the tenement at No. 5 underwent detailed and sympathetic restoration of the roof and external stonework under the direction of the architect Dennis Rodwell. The commemorative plaque was also taken from the north side of the building (the original front) and positioned on the south side where it can be seen from the pavement in Sciennes House Place. Restoration work was also carried out on the adjacent tenements at Nos. 7 and 9 by the architects Cameron and Gibb.

JEWISH BURIAL GROUND

ON THE SOUTH SIDE of Sciennes House Place, wedged between the former police station and a block of four-storey tenement buildings, is a tiny Jewish burial ground dating from 1816. This is also the year in which the first Congregation of Jews in Scotland was founded, with the Rev. Moses Joel as minister. Twenty families, living and working in Edinburgh, attended the first regular synagogue in a lane to the east of Nicolson Street, near the building presently occupied by St. Cuthbert's Co-operative Association.

Important dates in the establishment of the Jewish community in Edinburgh have, however, been recorded prior to 1816. According to *Silences That Speak*, by William Pitcairn Anderson, the first record of a Jewish burial in Edinburgh appears in the Town Council Minutes for 6th May 1795. Hermon Lyon, a dentist by profession, asked the Council for permission to create a burial place on Calton Hill for himself and his family, the place chosen being a natural cave or alcove on the north-west side of the hill. Permission was granted for a fee of £17 and a sepulchre with an iron gate was created in the natural alcove. The Minute of the Town Council runs as follows:

In a quiet corner of Sciennes House Place (formerly Braid Place), behind the old police station, is the Jewish Burial Ground, opened in 1816 and containing numerous headstones bearing Hebrew and Roman inscriptions. Photograph by Phyllis M. Cant.

Unto the Right Honourable the Lord Provost the Magistrates and Town Council of the City of Edinburgh . . . Humbly sheweth that your petitioner has for many years been an inhabitant of this City, and he hopes he has conducted himself in an orderly and peaceable manner. As he has been educated and brought up in Religious Tenets different from the established Religion of this country which on occasion of the death of himself or any of his family might prevent their remains from being interred in any of the consecrated burying grounds belonging to the City, he is most anxious to purchase a small plot of ground which he will inclose for a burying place for himself and family either on the land of Calton Hill or Bruntsfield links, as may be pointed out by your Honour's Overseer of Works.

Whilst there is no definite record of the number or dates of interments, it is believed that only Herman Lyon and his wife were ever buried there. As recently as 1931 the tomb was clearly recalled by the mother of Francis Caird Inglis who resided nearby at Rock House. The site was described as being on the slope beneath where the Observatory is, but when the path was being widened by the Council, the sepulchre, or most of it, was removed leaving only the back portion remaining. It is understood that on destruction of the sepulchre any memorial or remains were removed to the burial ground at Sciennes House Place.

As all the available ground at Sciennes was utilised by 1867, the Jewish community obtained new ground, firstly at Echo Bank Cemetery and then at Piershill. Of the twenty-nine separate stones at Sciennes, very few have inscriptions which can be fully deciphered. Most have Hebrew characters at the top and Roman characters beneath, all of which have been meticulously researched and recorded in *A History of the Origins of the First Jewish Community in Scotland – Edinburgh 1816*, by Abel Phillips. In 1925 the burial ground came under the control of Edinburgh Corporation but no records were passed over at that time.

At the present day, access is obtained either directly from Sciennes House Place when the gate is open, or through a rear door from the former police station in Causewayside.

CHAPTER 4

THE FEUING OF SCIENNES

To THE SOUTH OF MELVILLE DRIVE there is a large tract of land, roughly rectangular in shape, which originally formed part of the south bank of the Burgh Loch, until it was eventually drained at the beginning of the eighteenth century. In relation to modern street names this land is bounded, in the west by the lower half of Marchmont Crescent, in the east by the road called Sciennes, and on the south by Sciennes Road. Prior to 1860 there was a significant group of houses around Westerhall and New Campbeltown (now Roseneath and Argyle), and a greater concentration of population at Sciennes. Between these two, however, there were about half a dozen detached properties in large gardens which stretched from Melville Drive to Sciennes Road. Various feuing plans in the latter part of the nineteenth century greatly influenced the way in which different parts of the district developed.

The districts of Roseneath and Argyle were discussed at length in *Marchmont in Edinburgh* but a brief description of them is given here for completeness. Their origins are much more closely associated with the development of Sciennes than with the adjacent tenement district of Marchmont, with which they have become integrated. Marchmont was built on open farmland to a pre-determined feuing plan for Sir George Warrender of Bruntisfield House, whereas Roseneath and Argyle were developed piecemeal as the older properties of Westerhall and New Campbeltown deteriorated and became vacant.

55

ROSENEATH AND ARGYLE

THE COLOUR SHADING in *Bartholomew's Chronological Map of Edinburgh* suggests that parts of Roseneath date from at least 1622, but it is not until *Ainslie's Map* of 1804 that any substantial detail is available. Despite various developments over nearly two centuries, the position of modern-day streets follows closely the layout shown in *Ainslie's Map*. The whole district, now known as Roseneath and Argyle, contained little more than a dozen properties of various sizes, some of which were set in extensive grounds and ornamental gardens. Narrow access roads were the forerunners of Roseneath Street, Roseneath Place and Roseneath Terrace, between which were numerous paths or lanes leading to the houses. On the western extremity, beside Burntfield Links, one of the largest pieces of ground was owned by a Mr Martin whose house was situated on the south-west corner of his land, near what is now No. 1 Roseneath Place. To the east of Mr Martin's property lay a small group of houses, some of which still survive today. Between Roseneath Terrace and Roseneath Street a group of houses are shown, owned by Campbell and Dewar on the west side, with larger properties on the east side owned by Miss Warrender and Mr. Nasmith. The position of Argyle Place is marked by a single line of trees forming the east boundary of Nasmith's ground.

In the few years between *Ainslie's Map* of 1804 and *Kirkwood's Map* of 1817 considerable development took place. The most prominent change is the line of terraced houses Nos. 1 to 8 Meadow Place built around 1806 on land to the east of Mr. Martin's house. The group of houses to the north of the line of Roseneath Terrace are shown slightly differently, suggesting that Nos. 18 and 20 Meadow Place were built sometime between 1804 and 1817. Mr. Nasmith's land remains largely unchanged as do the houses to the west of it. Although neither *Ainslie's Map* of 1804 nor *Kirkwood's Map* of 1817 refers to the districts as New Campbeltown and

Victorine Foot working on one of her paintings in the studio, 1984. In the background are some of her late husband's sculpture. Courtesy of Victorine Foot (Mrs Schilsky).

Westerhall, there is no doubt that these names were used to denote the areas lying to the north and to the south of Roseneath Terrace.

The *Edinburgh and Leith Post Office Directory* began to include street maps of the city in 1828, but Roseneath and Argyle were not included until 1831. Minor developments can be traced in the succeeding two decades up to the time of the first *Ordnance Survey Map* of 1852. This map, perhaps more than any other, provides sufficient detail to gauge the general character of the district. Two communities are prominently marked: to the south, Westerhall abuts the estate of Sir George Warrender of Bruntisfield House; and to the north, the district of New Campbeltown (largely unnamed) lies between Westerhall and the Meadows. This quiet rural scene was home to several eminent citizens, artists and men of letters before the area succumbed to the tenement building era of the late nineteenth century.

The grandest house in Westerhall was Argyle Park built on land previously owned by Mr. Nasmith. It was acquired in 1821 by Duncan Stevenson, Deputy Lieutenant and Justice of the Peace for the County of Argyll, who came to Edinburgh from Oban around 1816. He printed and published the Tory-sponsored *Beacon* newspaper whose scurrilous attacks on James Stuart of Dunearn eventually led to a duel between Stuart and Sir Alexander Boswell of Auchinleck (son of Johnson's biographer), who was believed to be the instigator of the libel. The duel took place on 26th March 1822 at Auchtertool in Fife, as a result of which Boswell received a neck wound from which he died the following day. Stuart was charged with murder but was acquitted.

Somewhat less dramatic was the lifestyle of James Ballantine who lived at Warrender Lodge, immediately to the west of Argyle Park. Ballantine was a man of considerable talent, having been employed by the Royal Commissioners on the Fine Arts to execute the stained-glass windows for the House of Lords at Westminster. In addition to his profession as a glass-stainer he was author of several works including *The Miller of Deanhaugh* completed in 1845, set in the old Village of Dean towards the end of the eighteenth century. Another of Ballantine's works was *The Gaberlunzie's Wallet* of which *Chambers's Journal* said: 'The whole style is homely, but clever and decidedly original, arguing altogether an author who is of nobody's school or set'.

The intellectuals and men of learning of Westerhall also included Alexander Christie R.S.A., who lived at Westerhall Lodge in 1858. Christie started life as a law apprentice but later turned his attention to the world of art. In his formative years he studied under Sir William Allan and followed the tradition as a painter of historical subjects. Many of his subjects were taken from the novels of Sir Walter Scott, the life of Mary Queen of Scots and the Jacobite Rebellion. Little did Christie realise that this embryonic artists' colony was to be greatly expanded a few decades later, in neighbouring New Campbeltown. Patrick W. Adam was born in 1854 the son of an Edinburgh lawyer, but instead of following in the family tradition, Patrick decided to follow his love of art. He became a student at the Royal Scottish Academy, where he came under the influence of the leading Scottish painters of the day. He was elected an Associate of the Academy in 1883 and within a few years was sufficiently established to have a studio built for himself at New Campbeltown. It was here that he painted his series of Venetian pictures in 1889, amongst which were *The Ducal Palace* and *Santa Maria della Salute*, but it is generally considered that his most striking work was a number of winter landscapes completed about 1896. He gained the distinction of R.S.A. in 1897.

Although it is more than a century since Patrick Adam's studio was built, it has been used continuously over the years by several members of the art world, most notable amongst whom was Eric Schilsky, the sculptor. Eric Schilsky was born in Southampton on 22nd October 1898 into a musical family, his father being Charles Schilsky, the famous violinist and leader of Henry Wood's Queen's Hall Orchestra. However, it was in the world of art that Eric made his greatest impact. His early interest in art whilst at school in Geneva led later to the study of sculpture under Harvard Thomas at the Slade in London. He came to Edinburgh in 1945 as Head of the School of Sculpture at the Edinburgh College of Art, a post which he held until his retirement in 1969. In 1946 he married Victorine Foot, the painter, both artists working at the studio for many years until his death in 1974. The studio was converted in 1951 by the architect Alan Reiach to include residential accommodation. Since her husband's death, Victorine Foot has continued her work, maintaining the best traditions of the studio. Her paintings, which are varied and figurative, have been exhibited in the

Royal Academy and Royal Scottish Academy.

During his long lifetime Schilsky received many honours, being elected A.R.S.A. in 1952 and an Academician in 1956. The Royal Academy, London also elected him an Associate in 1957, and an Academician in 1968. He will probably be best remembered for a special quality which he brought to the art of sculpture and which is best described in his own words: 'a sensitive artist can make a good figure with little knowledge of anatomy but if he is not first an artist no amount of anatomical knowledge will help him'.

By 1870 Westerhall and New Campbeltown were beginning to feel vulnerable to the speculative builder. Much of the Grange had already been built, and on the adjacent Warrender estate a huge development of terraced houses was proposed by the Bryce Feuing Plan of 1869. On the other hand, Westerhall and New Campbeltown were redeveloped in a somewhat piecemeal fashion as existing properties were acquired over a period of almost thirty years from 1870. The resultant layout is less regimented, but from the historical point of view, more interesting in that several features remain from the pre-tenement era.

The largest uninterrupted tract of land was that on which Argyle Park stood, stretching from the Warrender estate boundary at the south end to Melville Drive at the north end. Argyle Park Terrace was designed in 1873 by the architect William Hamilton Beattie, whose later works included Jenners building in Princes Street. In Argyle Place, on the west side, five-storey Scottish baronial tenements were continued by the architect John C. Hay, the developer's plaque W.S. (William Steele) and the date 1875 being incorporated in the stonework at No. 42.

Meantime, in the lower half of Marchmont Crescent on the Warrender estate, a prolific builder, John Oliver, was constructing tenement buildings, from the rooftops of which he would have a bird's-eye view of the decaying houses below, in Westerhall and New Campbeltown. He was not

Looking north down Argyle Place, c. 1900. The terraced houses on the right date from 1860 and the tenement buildings on the left, built on the garden ground of Argyle Park, date from 1875.

long in realising their potential. He bought an old property, No. 16 Meadow Place (also previously owned by Stevenson the printer), from which he planned further development of the surrounding area. In 1884 he acquired Yew Tree House in Meadow Place Lane, which was demolished and replaced by the tenements Nos. 30 and 32 Roseneath Terrace and Nos. 19, 20 and 21 Roseneath Place. The following year he bought and demolished No. 17 Meadow Place for the construction of tenements and shops at Nos. 29 and 33 Roseneath Terrace and 16 Roseneath Place. Finally in 1886, after considerable local opposition to his first set of plans, the Dean of Guild Court approved the demolition of No. 16 Meadow Place which was replaced by Nos. 13, 14 and 15 Roseneath Place. The gap in the odd numbers of Roseneath Terrace (17 to 27 are missing) suggests that John Oliver may also have intended to demolish Nos. 19 and 20 Meadow Place. Fortunately these two early nineteenth-century semi-detached houses survive to this day, as do the walled lanes giving access to the remaining houses of New Campbeltown.

Westerhall survived a little longer, but the price paid was total extinction. Its principal houses were Warrender Lodge to the west of Argyle Park, Westerhall Lodge further to the west, Westerhall Cottage on the corner of what is now Roseneath Street and Roseneath Place, and Westerhall Villa in Roseneath Place just before the entrance to Roseneath Terrace. All these properties were cleared to make way for five-storey tenements and shops in Roseneath Terrace and Roseneath Place. They were designed in 1896 by the architect P. R. McLaren and constructed from a very hard, grey stone by the builder James Turner of No. 16 Torphichen Street, Edinburgh. The previous owners of Westerhall had long since fled the district, but even the flat-dwellers nearby objected to the line of the new buildings. Filed with the original plans is a letter to the Dean of Guild Court giving an interesting insight into the problems of the day:

> I take this liberty of drawing your attention to the plans for Tenements to be erected in Warrender Park Road (sic) adjoining ours. Our principal objection to this block is that instead of building it on a line with ours they intend to build out a few feet thus considerably shutting us in and obstructing and darkening our view. Also as the plans propose a fourth flat and shops on ground floor the symmetrical appearance of this side of street will be completely deranged. Regarding shops we may mention that there are already too many in the neighbourhood and some have stood empty since they were built (Marchmont Road) while others have had to be converted into houses, whereas main doors are in great demand and would be in keeping with the long rows of pretty main doors with plots in front which extend all along Warrender to the Links. Earnestly soliciting your interest in this.
>
> Signed, A *Proprietor.*

Unfortunately for the anonymous objector the plans went ahead without alteration, as a result of which the frontage of the tenement containing the shops comes out to the line of the bay windows of the earlier houses. Around the time of this development the old march wall between Westerhall and the Warrender estate was demolished, creating one street with two names: on the south side Warrender Park Road and on the north side Roseneath Street. The remaining section of the wall can still be seen, north of the police box and telephone box, dividing the lower half of Marchmont Crescent from Roseneath Place.

SYLVAN HOUSE

KIRKWOOD'S MAP OF 1817 shows Hugh Warrender as the owner of the property to the east of Westerhall. It is now occupied by the block of houses bounded by the east side of Argyle Place, Fingal Place, the west side of Sylvan Place, and the short stretch of Sciennes Road previously known as Carlung Place. Sources in *The Buildings of Scotland – Edinburgh* date houses in Fingal Place to 1825, in Sylvan Place to 1835, and on the east side of Argyle Place to 1860. By far the most interesting house in this block, however, is Sylvan House at No. 13 Sylvan Place, dating from before 1750 and now hidden from view by the tenement block Nos. 11 and 12 Sylvan Place. It is reached from a short lane at the south end of Sylvan Place and stands in its own garden, surrounded by houses of much more recent date. It is rectangular in shape, two storeys and attic in height, with an ornate door surround in sculptured stone. The whole house was sympathetically restored in 1983 by the present owners. The modern cement render was replaced with a lime harl, and internally many of the original features, including the staircase and the Baltic pine panelling, were retained. Removal of the old cement render on the external walls revealed that at some time in the past, the roof level had been raised to improve the attic accommodation. In addition, the early maps, c. 1817, show the house with a substantial wing to the east and entered by a driveway from the south, before the terraced houses were built at the west end of Sciennes Road. Despite the enormous amount of interest and attention given to Sylvan House over the years, it remains an enigma, as no conclusive evidence has yet been put forward to prove its age, nor the identity of the original owner. A well-researched article, by Margaret Tait, appeared in Volume XXX of the *Book of the Old Edinburgh Club* under the evocative title 'William's Hut'. The author advances the view that Sylvan House is the same house as 'William's Hut', 'erected by Joseph Williamson, advocate, upon the grounds of Leven Lodge'. The gist of the arguments and conclusions are contained in the following paragraph from the article:

> The history of William's Hut has never been disentangled from the voluminous and probably now incomplete title deeds of the various properties owned at one time or another by the Williamson family. It can only be asserted here that the titles of No. 13 Sylvan Place state that it was the house known as William's Hut 'erected by Joseph Williamson, advocate, upon the grounds of Leven Lodge'. It is therefore not to be confused with Leven Cottage, another small house much nearer to the parent property, which was built by the Earl of Leven at about the same date. My surmise is that before Joseph Williamson bought Leven Lodge itself in 1770 he had feued ground from the Earl and built William's Hut as a rural retreat for himself and his family.

Despite this article, Charles J. Smith, in *Historic South Edinburgh*, Volume 1, alludes to the doubt still expressed by certain local historians as to whether No. 13 Sylvan Place is, in fact, the original William's Hut. Whilst it is likely that in the absence of the full title deeds it may not be possible to

Sylvan House dating from between 1736 and 1750, believed to be 'William's Hut erected by Joseph Williamson, Advocate', and sympathetically restored in 1983 by the present owners. Photograph by Dale Idiens.

prove the matter conclusively, certain additional information has recently come to light from an unexpected source.

In 1881 Town and Country Heritable Trust Ltd. acquired an interest in the ground on which Sylvan House stood, with a view to future development. Four years later they applied to the Dean of Guild Court for a warrant to make alterations at *No. 11* Sylvan Place, 'to take down the Eastmost house on their property at Sylvan Place, to make alterations on east gable of the Westmost house and to erect new double tenement fronting Sylvan Place, consisting of four floors and containing in all 16 dwelling houses with boundary walls, drains etc.'. The reference to their property as *No. 11* must have been either to the eastmost part of Sylvan House which was to be demolished, or alternatively to the eastmost and westmost parts together. When the tenement was built in 1885 it was numbered 11 and 12 and the remaining part of Sylvan House was numbered 13. But for the intervention of the next-door neighbour the story might have ended there. Mr. Scott, at No. 10, suddenly found that his open outlook and view of Sylvan House would be blocked by the intended four-storey tenement building. Through his solicitor he raised a number of complaints designed to safeguard the amenity of his property, which meant that the Dean of Guild Court was compelled to consider a large number of documents tracing the ownership of the land on which the buildings stood. From the list of fifty productions it is possible to trace every transaction from 1734 to 1881 when Town and Country Heritable Trust Ltd. obtained their interest. None of these documents refers to Joseph Williamson. There are, however, numerous references to persons whose interest in the land on which Sylvan House was built can be proved easily from other sources, notably Sir James Johnstone of Westerhall in 1734 and Sir George Warrender in 1813. In searching for a connection with Joseph Williamson of 'William's Hut' it is difficult to escape the observation that the person who owned Sylvan House for the longest period (1763 to 1791) was *William* Henry Doig, whose nephew fell heir to the house on the death of William in 1791. The nephew, described as 'James Doig of the Island of Antigua', did not take up residence but sold the property in 1792 to Walter Riddel. A further recent reference to Sylvan House tends to fit this pattern of events: an article by R. G. W. Anderson in *A Hotbed of Genius* identifies Sylvan House as the summer retreat in the 1790s of Dr Joseph Black, Professor of Chemistry at Edinburgh University.

The Dean of Guild papers do not disprove the William's Hut theory but they do make proof of it from some other source that bit more desirable. The absence of Williamson's name from the list could be explained if ownership of Sylvan House devolved differently to the two and a half acres of land on which it was built. Margaret Tait in her article in the *Book of the Old Edinburgh Club* states that 'the Edinburgh Directories have provided no information about previous

Sciennes Road (formerly Sciennes Loaning) which originally gave access to the large houses known collectively as Hope Park. They were progressively demolished in the late nineteenth century, one of the few remaining links being the house now occupied by the janitor of Sciennes School. Photograph by Phyllis M. Cant.

occupants'. If the reference to 'Edinburgh Directories' includes the *Edinburgh and Leith Post Office Directories*, they do, in fact, provide useful information although not listed under Sylvan House or Sylvan Place. From 1841 to 1845 Lt.-Col. David Williamson is shown as residing at No. 6 Hope Park, and it is beyond doubt that this was the address of Sylvan House when the houses of Hope Park were numbered from the east end of Sciennes Loaning. Margaret Tait provides the last piece in the jigsaw herself when she concludes her article by saying that William's Hut was inherited by Joseph Williamson's grandson, Lt.-Col. David Williamson.

The Dean of Guild papers are also helpful in establishing the date of Sylvan House. One of the documents relating to the sale of the land, dated 15th February 1750, refers for the first time to the existence of a dwelling house 'built by the said James Hamilton', and it is known that Hamilton bought the land on 22nd July 1736 although he did not get a Charter of Confirmation from Sir James Johnstone of Westerhall until 1739. The inference, therefore, is that Sylvan House was built sometime between 1736 and 1750, but perhaps after 1739.

Sylvan Place to Gladstone Terrace

IN THE EARLY NINETEENTH CENTURY the area from the east side of Sylvan Place to Gladstone Terrace was divided into four plots of unequal size with one large house and several outbuildings on each parcel of land. Without exception, the houses lay to the south of the plot near Sciennes Loaning (now Sciennes Road) with entrances in some cases from the north and the south. Generally the ornamental part of the garden was on the south side, suggesting that the main entrance was from Sciennes Loaning, with the longer part of the garden running down to Melville Drive.

The first plot to the east is the site now occupied by the Royal Edinburgh Hospital for Sick Children, opened in 1895. In 1817 the property, then known as Rillbank, belonged to William Wilson, whose large L-shaped house sat amidst extensive ornamental gardens and shrubberies. An entrance gate and short driveway came in from Sciennes Loaning, and a much longer and narrower driveway lay to the north. This property was greatly altered in 1855 when it was purchased by the governors of the Trades Maiden Hospital, which had outgrown its previous accommodation at Argyle Square. Shortly after the Trades Maiden Hospital came to Rillbank the north part of the feu was surveyed for building development as a result of which the streets of Rillbank were built in the early 1860s.

The second feu to the east of Sylvan House is that on which Sciennes School was built in 1890. Boog Watson traces extracts from the title deeds dated 17th August 1734 which confirm the sale of four acres of land by Sir James Johnstone of Westerhall to Andrew Gairdner, brewer in Burrowloch, and his spouse Cecilia Stewart. With the assistance of the early nineteenth-century maps, and the ground plan prepared by the school's architect, it is possible to reconstruct the nature of the locality with reasonable accuracy. The feu, stretching from Sciennes Loaning to Melville Drive, was almost completely bounded by lines of mature trees. The principal house, owned by George Miller from 1800, was L-shaped and stood at the south end of the feu. It was reached by a curving driveway from the south, and a long narrow driveway from the north, close to the eastmost boundary. As the Miller family owned the property for almost the whole of the nineteenth century, it is difficult to know why an advertisement for sale appeared in the *Edinburgh Leith Glasgow and North British Commercial Advertiser* for 15th November 1828, but it does give a good description of the property:

> Advertisement of public roup by Watson's Trustees of W. enclosure with Mansion House and offices built thereon (No. 4 Hope Park) being part of the four acres sometime ago feued by Andrew Gardner late brewer at Burrowloch from Sir James Johnston of Westerhall Bart., and now possessed by Mr. Wm. Miller. House contains dining and drawing rooms with nine sleeping apartments besides kitchen, servants bedroom scullery and cellar, stables, gardener's house, a wash house and a variety of other offices, one of which has been a coach house — kitchen garden fruit garden and shrubbery with park in front of the house.

The latter part of this advertisement may have related to a group of buildings almost abutting Sciennes Loaning, although they were specifically excluded from the conveyance to George Miller in 1800. They were described in the 1877 *Ordnance Survey Map* as Woodhead Place and were numbered 1 to 4 Woodhead Place in the *Edinburgh and Leith Post Office Directory* between 1868 and 1889. Alterations were probably made to them shortly after the main entrance to the principal house was changed to the north, via Millerfield Place which was built in 1864.

When Robert Wilson, architect to the School Board, came to draw ground plans for Sciennes School in 1890, he included a most interesting plan of the intended school building superimposed on a ground plan of the old house and Woodhead Place. This shows quite clearly that Miller's house stood exactly where the south-east frontage of Sciennes School now stands, and that Woodhead Place would have been a few feet into the boys' playground. The original intention was to demolish Woodhead Place and Miller's house. At the end of 1889 the Dean of Guild Court was asked to approve plans for the main school, which included a house for the janitor in the girls' playground near the boundary with the Trades Maiden Hospital. The intended two-storey house, facing south, was of a most elaborate design, almost square in shape, with a large, stone-mullioned bay window to the front. The steeply pitched roof was pierced by high stone chimneys and topped by ornamental ironwork along the ridge. Perhaps on account of rising costs, the proposed house for the janitor was abandoned and instead Robert Wilson was asked to look again at the possibility of utilising part of Woodhead Place. The greatest problem was that if the buildings were not removed they would obstruct the area around the gate to the boys' playground. Wilson therefore proposed the demolition of Nos. 3 and 4 and the westmost part of the semi-detached block. The remaining eastmost house was given a new gable wall and additional facilities. The result was the janitor's house as it is seen today, clearly showing alterations to the roof line and having a west gable in different stone to the remainder of the house. This house is virtually the only

70

Beside Melville Drive a low retaining wall and numerous gate pillars mark the north boundary of the original feus on Sciennes Loaning (now Sciennes Road). Through the gateway, to the north, lay the Burgh Loch, now occupied by the Meadows. Photograph by Phyllis M. Cant.

remaining part of the small estate of George Miller, the father of William Miller the famous engraver, both of whom lived at Sciennes in the nineteenth century.

The story of the Miller family has been recorded by several eminent writers on Edinburgh, notably by John G. Gray in *The South Side Story* and more recently by Charles J. Smith in Volume 3 of *Historic South Edinburgh*. George Miller came from a long-established Quaker family in Edinburgh whose ancestors included the hereditary master gardener at Holyroodhouse, the famous seedsman at the Canongate, and the owner of Craigentinny Castle. The latter's son, William Henry Miller, earned himself the nickname 'Measure Miller' from his eccentric habit of visiting various book sales and measuring precisely the size of each volume before deciding if it would enhance his existing collection. Details of his peculiar lifestyle and interment below the Craigentinny Marbles are related in the Restalrig chapter of *Villages of Edinburgh*, Volume 1.

George Miller, father of the engraver, was born near Holyroodhouse and was educated at the High School under Dr Adams. He started in business as a shawl manufacturer in Bristo Street, later moving to a house on the corner of Drummond Street and Nicolson Street, where his son William was born on 28th May 1796. In 1800 he moved to the large country house built on the ground now occupied by Sciennes School. Several writers have referred to the name of the house as Hope Park and later Millerfield House. Whilst there is no reason to suggest that the name Hope Park was not used to denote Miller's own house, it was also used to describe that rectangular tract of land stretching from present-day Gladstone Terrace to the east side of Argyle Place. The houses in Hope Park were numbered from the east side, making Miller's house No. 4 and Sylvan House No. 6. This information was obviously not available to the author of an article entitled 'Edinburgh Engravers' in Volume IX of the *Book of the Old Edinburgh Club*, who stated that 'Miller lived first at 4 Hope Park and thereafter at Millerfield House, Millerfield Place'. The two descriptions refer, in fact, to the same house.

It was probably intended that William Miller follow his father into the family business but instead he took up an apprenticeship in engraving with William Archibald in Edinburgh, and later in London with George Cook. When he returned to Edinburgh in 1821 he set up his studio in Hope Park and was not long in establishing a reputation for high-class work. He also held popular classes in engraving, one of his pupils being Sir Daniel Wilson, author of *Memorials of Edinburgh in the Olden Time*. During his long life Miller produced an almost endless list of accomplishments in the world of engraving, catalogued in 1886 under the title *A Catalogue of Engravings by William Miller A.R.S.A. 1818 to 1871*. One of his earliest works, in 1826, was an engraving of *Lauriston Castle* after a drawing by James Skene, followed by three works based on Turner, namely *Edinburgh from Blackford Hill 1831; Edinburgh from St. Anthony's Chapel 1836;* and *Craigmillar Castle 1836*. A further Edinburgh scene was *Edinburgh from Arthur's Seat 1845* after H. W. Williams. In addition to several other works by Turner, Miller engraved drawings by Sir George Harvey, President of the Royal Scottish Academy. Included is Harvey's Disruption picture, *Leaving the Manse*, which reproduces part of the garden of Hope Park. He also engraved illustrations for the novels of Sir Walter Scott; Lockhart's *Life of Scott;* Dr John Brown's *Rab and His Friends;* and works of poetry by Thomas Campbell and Samuel Rogers.

In addition to his very full life as an expert engraver he spent much of his time in support of the Quakers, involving himself with the great crusades of the day, the Peace Society and the Edinburgh Society for the Abolition of Slavery. In the last decade of his life he retired from business and spent much of his time painting watercolours, but he remained at Hope Park to which he had been brought at the age of four by his father. There have been many tributes to the work of William Miller but perhaps the one which best sums up his life at Hope Park is that by Sir Daniel Wilson, eminent author and admiring pupil:

> His studio and hospitable mansion stood till recently at Millerfield, on the south side of the Meadows, though hemmed in with the encroaching town, where in his own early years an unobstructed view commanded Arthur Seat and the Pentland Hills. A sundial of fine proportions and artistic beauty of detail formed a conspicuous feature in the garden, with a motto from Horace, *Odes* Book IIxiv
>
> 'Eheu fugaces, Posthume, Posthume,
> Labuntur anni'.
>
> It was carved from his own design, and its dial-plate engraved by himself, and remained as it was set up by

him in the centre of the old-fashioned parterre, with its winding paths and quaint boxwood edgings: the haunt from earliest youth of the gentle, gifted artist, who retained his faculties in full vigour to the close, in his eighty-sixth year, of a life of unostentatious benevolence and unwearied devotion to art.

William Miller died on 20th January 1882 during a visit to his daughter in Sheffield. He was interred in the burial ground of the Society of Friends Meeting House in the Pleasance among his Quaker ancestors.

The last two feus of ground at Hope Park were those on which Livingstone Place and Gladstone Terrace were built between 1865 and 1869. The westmost feu (Livingstone Place) was about half the width of the Gladstone Terrace feu, but of the same length. In the early nineteenth century the old mansion on the narrow feu was owned by Bailie Louden and later by Walter Lothian. It was set fairly far back from Sciennes Loaning and was flanked by large symmetrical buildings to the east and west. Altogether the site was very detailed and geometric in lay-out, with the driveway approaching along the east boundary from a small lodge house and gate pillars on Sciennes Loaning. Immediately opposite the lodge house a narrow road (in the approximate position of Tantallon Place) led to Grange Farm. When Bailie Louden's house was demolished, the feu was developed independently of the Gladstone Terrace feu. The restricted site meant that Livingstone Place was built as a very narrow street with short front gardens and small backgreens on both sides of the street. The entire feu on which Bailie Louden's house sat is now marked by the backgreen walls on the east and west sides of Livingstone Place. Construction of four-storey tenement buildings commenced about 1868 at the north-east end but it was not until the following year that the west side was begun. Unfortunately, detailed plans for the street are not available

Alasdair Alpin MacGregor, the author, with his 'Golden Lamp' in the house of his landlady Miss Jane Aitken at No. 12 Gladstone Terrace. Among his Edinburgh titles were *Auld Reekie*, *The Turbulent Years* and *The Golden Lamp*. Photograph from *The Golden Lamp* published by Michael Joseph Ltd.

as the authority of the Dean of Guild Court did not extend south of the Meadows until the 1870s. The houses, however, do not display any of the architectural interest associated with the larger flats of Warrender Park Road or Marchmont Road.

The feu on which Gladstone Terrace was built was owned by James Tod in the early nineteenth century. *Kirkwood's Map* of 1817 shows two fairly substantial detached properties at the south-east corner, reached by a driveway from Sciennes Loaning and from the north. At the south end of the driveway there was a lodge house and other small outbuildings. The property was numbered 1 and 2 Hope Park from at least 1833. However, its development in the mid-1860s was slightly more complicated than at Livingstone Place a few years later. After the old buildings were cleared from the site, several ideas were put forward for utilising the full breadth of the feu. One idea, in 1865, was to build Gladstone Terrace very wide at the north end, and allow it to branch out into an elegant crescent where it met Sciennes Road. At least one map shows one of the original houses still retained in the island formed by the intended new crescent and the north side of Sciennes Road. However, the plan was abandoned and by 1866 Gladstone Terrace was a single broad street running north to south with houses built on the east side. By the following year the west side, Nos. 11 to 18, was built, completing a very broad well-proportioned street with long front gardens and large backgreens.

The extensive area of ground on which Nos. 1 to 6 Hope Park were laid out in the eighteenth century remained largely unchanged until the house-building era of the late nineteenth century. It was only then that the quiet rural scene was threatened and eventually destroyed when the last two feus were developed for Sciennes School and the Royal Edinburgh Hospital for Sick Children. Today the area is settled in terms of housing development but still retains some evidence of the original plan. Some early nineteenth-century property remains at Roseneath with Sylvan House (and probably the janitor's house) dating from the mid-eighteenth century. Only one other link remains — not generally appreciated by the many people who traverse the district each day. Beside the pedestrian walk on the south side of Melville Drive an old crumbling stone wall has been progressively reduced in height as the roadway has been resurfaced in Melville Terrace, Rillbank Crescent and Fingal Place. This wall is the original north boundary of the Hope Park properties. Several openings have been blocked up and others have been realigned to suit the position of the streets coming down from Sciennes Road. The different heights in the wall, however, match exactly the north-south boundaries between the old houses of Hope Park. Whilst it is impossible to be certain, the individually designed gate pillars, which obviously pre-date the tenement era, probably marked the north entrance to each of the principal houses.

One of these principal houses was owned by the father of Henry Cockburn (1779–1854) who described the house in *Memorials of His Time* as 'the eastmost house on the south side of the Meadows' where Cockburn spent most of his schooldays and early youth. In his *Memorials* Lord Cockburn makes frequent mention of the ruined Convent, the village of Sheens, the Grange Estate and Sir Andrew Lauder and his family.

Long after Lord Cockburn's father's house had been demolished and after Gladstone Terrace had been in existence for more than half a century Alasdair Alpin MacGregor lived at No. 12 with his landlady Miss Jane Aitken. Among his Edinburgh books were *Auld Reekie*, *The Turbulent Years* and *The Golden Lamp*.

CHAPTER 5

THE FEUING
OF THE GRANGE

THE GRANGE WAS FEUED AND DEVELOPED in quite a different way to Sciennes, Westerhall and New Campbeltown. Grange House was the focal point of the estate, which was almost completely farmland in 1825 when Sir Thomas Dick-Lauder first considered the idea of feuing out parts of his estate for building. From the outset he had control over the manner in which the ground would be feued, and the character of the neighbourhood which he wished to create. Above all, his plans were greatly simplified by the fact that there were very few houses on the estate of any significance, which were not associated with the estate or farm. Whilst there can be no doubt that farm workers would be decanted from their cottages, building progress was not impeded by legal wrangles over ownership of the land or the protection of other people's property rights.

Against that background feuing plans were produced fairly quickly by well-known architects of the day and each phase of building was completed without undue delay. In the event, several feuing plans were produced before the whole area of the Grange was built.

VARIOUS FEUING PLANS

SOME IDEA OF THE RURAL CHARACTER OF THE GRANGE can be obtained by studying the Estate Plan of the Grange, dated 1760, preserved at West Register House. The plan is not to scale, but its more prominent features can easily be related to

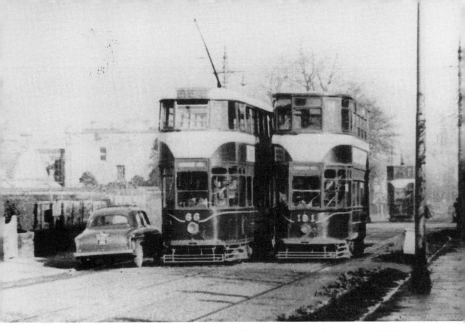

Grange Road begins to show signs of traffic congestion as early as 1950 with service No. 6 (Marchmont Circle) going down and service No. 14 (Granton Circle) coming up.

the layout of existing streets. The estate was bounded, on the north, by the 'Public Road from back of the Meadows to Sheens' (now Sciennes Road), and on the south by 'Grange loan joining the Road to Libberton'. On the east, the boundary adjoined the feus at Causewayside, and, on the west, the separate estates of Whitehouse and Bruntisfield. This west boundary is now marked by a line east of Kilgraston Road and the backgreen wall of the east side of Marchmont Crescent. The estate, almost square in shape, was divided by three 'roads', one running due east and west, and the other two, more or less, north and south. The 'Dean of Guild's walk' ran east to west near the line of what became Dick Place, and 'The Kirk road through Bruntsfield Links' ran north to south, on what is now Lovers' Loan. The remaining thoroughfare was a 'cart road' southwards from Sheens, which passed to the east of Grange Farm and crossed Dean of Guild's Walk, before joining Grange Loan. The cart road is not identifiable with any modern street, but was approximately along the line of Tantallon Place and Cumin Place.

Grange House lay in the south-west corner of the estate, a few yards south of Dean of Guild's Walk.

The estate remained more or less undeveloped until 1825 when Sir Thomas Dick-Lauder decided to feu out parts of the ground for building. As the estate was entailed (restricted to a designated line of heirs), it was necessary for Sir Thomas to obtain an Act of Parliament to give him the necessary powers. The Act was passed in 1825 'to enable Sir Thomas Dick Lauder, Baronet and the heirs of entail succeeding to him in the Estate of Grange to grant feus thereof upon certain terms and conditions'. These terms and conditions, which formed an integral part of each feuing plan, were fairly onerous, designed to maintain a high standard in the layout of the streets, the design of the houses, the value of the properties, and the exclusion of all development other than for residential use. The first feuing plan was prepared in 1825 for Sir Thomas by Grainger and Miller. It consisted of a geometric grid of the intended main streets superimposed on the existing fields. Grange Road was stopped at Lovers' Loan with Dick Place to the south extending the full width of the estate. These two main thoroughfares were joined by Mansionhouse Road, Lauder Road (which extended to Grange Loan) and Cumin Place.

The 1825 Feuing Plan was followed by David Cousin's Plan of 1851, details of which were advertised in *The Scotsman* on 14th February 1852 in a lengthy announcement, part of which stated that:

> There will be exposed to Feu, by Public Auction within the Salerooms of Messrs. Cay & Black, No. 45 George Street, Edinburgh, upon Monday the 8th day of March 1852, at Twelve O'clock noon, THOSE PORTIONS of the ENTAILED ESTATE of GRANGE, consisting of ninety-three Lots, laid out for Feus, as the same are delineated on a Feuing Plan, prepared by David Cousin, Esq., Architect, Edinburgh, and situated in the Roads or Streets called, or to be called, The Mansion-House Road; Dick Place; The Lauder

Kilravock, designed by David MacGibbon, c. 1874, for Hugh Rose Jnr., of Craig and Rose, Leith. It became St. Raphael's Hospital at the end of the First World War. Courtesy of the Little Company of Mary.

Road; The Grange Loan; Cumin Place; The Grange Road; Tantallon Place, and Hatton Place — all lying within . . .

For further particulars apply to David Cousin, Esq., Architect, Royal Exchange, Edinburgh; or to Messrs Scott, Rymer & Scott, Chambers, No. 38 North Frederick Street, Edinburgh; either of whom will show the feuing plan and articles of roup.

Edinburgh, 27th January 1852

Cousin modified the 1825 Plan in some important aspects. Whilst he retained the general layout, he introduced some curved streets (Tantallon Place, St. Catherine's Place and Dalrymple Crescent) and altered others (Lauder Road) in order to soften the geometric lines of the first plan. He also restricted the layout of Dick Place, at the east end by stopping it at Findhorn Place, and at the west end by turning it short of the west boundary of the estate. Before Kilgraston Road was built he intended Dick Place to turn in a right angle and proceed southwards to meet Grange Loan.

To complete the estate two other feuing plans were produced in 1858 and 1864, this time by Robert Reid Raeburn. Unfortunately, of all the feuing plans done for the Grange only Raeburn's 1864 Plan survives. Nevertheless, the development of the district can be plotted from the various *Ordnance Survey Maps* and the *Edinburgh and Leith Post Office Directories*. Maps were first included in the *Edinburgh and Leith Post Office Directories* in 1828 but it was not until 1835 that the area covered as far south as the Grange. The 1852 map provides significant detail. The main east to west streets were Hatton Place, Grange Road (stopping at Grange Cemetery) and Dick Place, and the north to south streets were Mansionhouse Road, Lauder Road, Tantallon Place, St. Catherine's Place, Seton Place and Findhorn Place. No streets were developed south of Grange Loan.

Raeburn's Feuing Plan of 1864 shows the Grange at an advanced stage of planning, but still with significant gaps, and some interesting ideas which were never implemented. All the main roads were formed, and named, with Grange House shielded from view by plantations of trees on all four sides. Grange Farm was cut off by new streets and lay within the rectangle formed by Grange Road, Cumin Place, Dick Place and Lauder Road. The road which connected Grange House to Grange Farm was stopped halfway along its length and emerged at a new entrance on the corner of Dick Place and Lauder Road. Dick Place was extended, at its west end, to cross the boundary into the Whitehouse Estate where Kilgraston Road, Blackford Road and Hope Terrace were laid out. South of Grange Loan there were no houses, other than West Grange and isolated farm dwellings, but streets were formed between Grange Terrace and West Relugas Road.

The least developed part of the estate was within the rectangle bounded by Hatton Place, Tantallon Place, Grange Road and the east boundary of the Bruntisfield Estate. The

Blackford Farm and Station at the junction of Blackford Avenue and Charterhall Road 1890. The only surviving building is the farmhouse on the north side of the railway line. From the Yerbury Collection.

intended layout of the area now occupied by Chalmers Crescent and Palmerston Road was quite different to what was eventually built. Middle Meadow Walk was to be extended southwards, west of Argyle Place, to open out into a Y-shaped avenue to the Southern Cemetery. Raeburn also included designation S for areas which he intended to be occupied by shops and flats. One of these areas was the north side of Hatton Place and the other was the north side of Grange Road between what is now Beaufort Road and Mansionhouse Road. In the event, no shops or flats were included until Marchmont was built in the 1870s.

Raeburn's third feuing plan, in 1877, was confined to the area south of Grange Loan. It required alteration to the flow of the Pow Burn for the construction of the Suburban and South Side Junction Railway, and West Relugas Road.

THE FIRST RESIDENTS

AS HOUSES WERE COMPLETED and families moved in, the

increase of population was recorded, fairly accurately, in the *Edinburgh and Leith Post Office Directories*. As the *Directory* was entirely voluntary it did not necessarily include every family, nor the exact date of residence. Nevertheless, the information is interesting, particularly in a street which is reasonably representative of the district. Entries began for Dick Place in 1853 with Asbury Villa (later shown as Ashbury Villa) owned by Mrs Touch. By 1859 there were fifteen entries, which had doubled by 1861 when house numbering was introduced, starting from the east end. Prior to that, and for many years after, most houses had individual names: Iona Villa; Cawdor Villa; East Villa; Woodbine Cottage; Bellevue Lodge; and many others. Among the occupations mentioned were ministers of religion, accountants, solicitors, architects, a portrait painter, and a professor of music, as well as representatives of well-known family businesses in Edinburgh. This latter group included: James Dowell of Dowell & Lyon, Auctioneers; James Middlemass of Middlemass Biscuits; and G. Boyd Thornton of Thornton & Co., Waterproof and India Rubber Manufacturers of 78 Princes Street. The rather quaint description of the businesses is also evident from the entries for two close neighbours, Thomas Knox and Duncan Cameron. Thomas Knox was a principal in Knox, Samuel and Dickson, Fringe and Gimp Manufacturers, Hosiers, Glovers, Lace and Berlin Wool Manufacturers, Jewellers and Perfumers who had retail premises in Hanover Street and a factory at Mound Place. Duncan Cameron was the owner of the famous Wholesale Stationer and Steel Pen Patentee, whose advertising board still exists at Blair Street, near the Tron Church:

> They come as a Boon and a Blessing to men
> The Pickwick, the Owl and the Waverley Pen.

Most of the houses in Dick Place were built in similar-sized feus, although there was great variety in the architecture. There were one or two notably larger feus with correspondingly grander buildings, particularly on the south side of the street. Among these were Egremont or Park House, built by

Oswald House designed by Robert Morham for James Buchanan, the chemist, of Duncan Flockhart. The house was built in 1876 and extended to the east in 1880. In the garden are the extensive peach houses, orchid houses and vineries. The house was demolished c. 1970 and the site developed as Oswald Court, off Oswald Road. Courtesy of Miss Jean Smart.

the architect F. T. Pilkington for his own use, Craigmount, used as a Boys' School from 1865, and Esdaile, now the Training School of the Royal Bank of Scotland. Further afield the development was equally grand, including Monkwood in Kilgraston Road, Dunard and Ashfield in Grange Loan, South Park (now the British Geological Survey) and Kilravock (now St. Raphael's) in Blackford Avenue, and Blackford Brae and Blackford Park at the west end of South Oswald Road.

Only occasionally does the span of human memory reach into the nineteenth century, but when it does, it is possible to reconstruct at least something of the day-to-day life of a family living in one of these large detached villas. Oswald House was built in 1876 in Oswald Road for James

Buchanan, an eminent chemist with the Edinburgh firm of Duncan Flockhart. He started as a young apprentice, and worked up to be a principal in the firm, and an acknowledged expert in the use of various plants for pharmaceutical preparations. Many of these plants were grown and nurtured in Duncan Flockhart's own physic garden at Warriston.

Oswald House was built on a very extensive feu, on an end site, which stretched from Oswald Road down to South Oswald Road. The house was built at the north end of the feu to take maximum advantage of the long, south-facing garden on which there were several greenhouses. These were laid out as orchid houses and also for growing a wide range of semi-exotic plants including peaches, figs, vines and palms. The remaining garden was still large enough to contain lawns, shrubberies and a bowling green, which could be flooded in the winter for curling. To the south of the formal garden lay a large walled vegetable garden, the gardener's cottage, and a small observatory used in connection with Mr Buchanan's interest in amateur astronomy. The original two-storey house, designed by Buchanan's brother-in-law, Robert Morham (who also designed Marchmont St. Giles Church), had several bedrooms with the principal public rooms and the library to the south. As Mr & Mrs Buchanan's family increased — eventually to nine children, one of whom died in infancy — a large extension was built in 1880 to the east of the house. This almost doubled the available space to include additional bedrooms, a large nursery with a separate flight of steps to the garden, and accommodation for the cook, the nurse and maidservants. There was no stable in the garden ground at Oswald House. The coachman, Matthew Keddie, kept the horses at Duncan Street and would appear each morning to take Mr Buchanan to Duncan Flockhart's and return for him at lunchtime and at the end of the day. Between these times, Matthew would also need to fit in numerous other journeys, to take Mrs Buchanan into town or to take the many children to visit their friends. In summer an open landau was used and, in the winter, a brougham. Of the six daughters, most of them

James Buchanan of Oswald House had this substantial house built for his gardener on the corner of Oswald Road and South Oswald Road. Photograph by Phyllis M. Cant.

attended school locally, at Bell's Academy in Lauder Road and later Craigmount in Dick Place, whereas the two sons travelled into the city centre for their education. Each Sunday, all the family and the staff attended 'Uncle Robert's church' (Grange Parish Church, later Marchmont St. Giles) to hear the first minister, the Rev. William L. Riach, preach.

James Buchanan died in March 1909 at the age of seventy-eight and was buried in Grange Cemetery. The family lived on in Oswald House until 1922 when Mrs Buchanan and five of her children moved to No. 13 Lauder Road. Mrs Buchanan died in 1931. As the family unit dwindled, the inscriptions on the family tomb lengthened, until the last member, Margaret Buchanan, died on 20th May 1988 in her ninety-eighth year. But for her acute faculties, retained to the end of her life, some of the Buchanan story might never have been recorded. When the house in Lauder Road was sold, many of the children's toys which had lain in the attics for decades were presented to the Museum of Childhood in the High Street, Edinburgh.

Oswald House remained in private occupation until the outbreak of the Second World War when it was requisitioned by the War Office. At the end of the War it became an Eventide Home for blind ladies, run by The Royal Blind Asylum, who remained there until the residents were transferred to the Thomas Burns Home in Alfred Place in 1969. Oswald House was sold, demolished and replaced by a quadrangle of houses, retaining only the distinctive gate pillars of James Buchanan's original house.

ARCHITECTS

THE CONSTRUCTION OF THE GRANGE attracted several architects of the highest calibre, in addition to Robert Morham, some of whom found the district sufficiently attractive to set up their own homes there. A well-researched section in *The Grange — A Case for Conservation* is devoted to this subject, the architects being listed in chronological order of their date of death.

One of the best known was David Bryce (1803–1876) whose most prominent city buildings include the Royal Infirmary and the redesigned Bank of Scotland on the Mound. He was heavily committed to the development of the Bruntisfield Estate for Sir George Warrender but his plan was abandoned after his death in 1876. Had his plan been implemented, Marchmont would have been built with detached houses, similar to the Grange, in Marchmont Road and Marchmont Crescent, and three-storey terraced houses in Warrender Park Road, and Terrace. Bryce also designed Grange Cemetery which was opened in 1847 as the Edinburgh Southern Cemetery.

David Cousin (1809–1878) was one of the architects who chose to live in the locality of the Grange, having built No. 7 Greenhill Gardens, in 1849, for his own use. His public works, as Edinburgh City Architect, included large-scale clearances of the medieval Old Town and replacement

The McCallum tomb, one of many fine examples of sculpture in Grange Cemetery first laid out in 1847 by the Edinburgh Southern Cemetery Co. Ltd. Photograph by Phyllis M. Cant.

with habitable dwellings fitted with proper sanitation. He designed the Edinburgh University Reid School of Music at Bristo, and reconstructed James Court in the Lawnmarket after it had been seriously damaged by fire. In the Grange, Cousin was responsible for the second feuing plan dated 1851.

The architect who probably had most to do with the feuing plans, rather than the designs of individual houses in the Grange, was Robert Reid Raeburn (1819~1888) whose plans were drawn in 1858, 1864 and 1877. His obvious flair for seeing potential development in the old estates nearest to Edinburgh eventually earned him several important commissions. Among his designs for individual houses were Rosetta in Inverleith Gardens and Dunard in Grange Loan. He also designed the tenements and shops in Grange Road, opposite Salisbury Church.

As well as being an accomplished architect, Sir James

Gowans (1821–1890) was involved in many public projects, notably his planning of the International Exhibition of Industry, Science and Art held in the West Meadows in 1886. Part of the exhibition was his model tenements for working-class families constructed in the north-east corner of the Meadows near the Infirmary. He designed the commemorative pillars at the west end of Melville Drive, probably two houses in Mansionhouse Road and the tall flats with crown-capped towers in Castle Terrace. Perhaps his most unusual building was his own house, Rockville, at No. 3 Napier Road, nicknamed 'the Pagoda', which was demolished in 1966. Sir James Gowans was buried in the Grange Cemetery, his grave marked by a large tomb set against the north boundary wall.

Not all the architects working in the Grange were local to Edinburgh. Frederick Thomas Pilkington (1832–1898) was born in Lincolnshire although he graduated from Edinburgh University and set up in practice in Edinburgh. By far his most striking work in the Grange was his own house Egremont (later renamed Grange Park House), followed by Craigmount, both in Dick Place. Nos. 48 and 50 Dick Place are also by Pilkington, as are 129 and 131 Grange Loan, although the last two are more restrained examples of his usual flamboyant style. Beyond the Grange, Pilikington's most prominent buildings include the Barclay Church and Craigend Park, Liberton.

Hippolyte Jean Blanc (1844–1917) was one of Edinburgh's great church architects. He designed Mayfield Church, Christ Church at Holy Corner, and Cluny Church (formerly St. Matthew's) at Morningside Station. He lived for many years at No. 17 Strathearn Place, now occupied by the Iona Hotel. A tenement building at Nos. 21–25 Marchmont Road was designed by Blanc but unfortunately most of the intricate work was omitted during building in 1880.

Three more modern architects are also worthy of mention: Sir R. Rowand Anderson (1835–1920) designed the McEwan Hall and also Masson Hall in South Lauder Road; John Kinross (1855–1931) built three very striking

90

Carlton Cricket Club at the Grange, c. 1889. From the Yerbury Collection.

houses in Mortonhall Road, one for his own use; and George Washington Browne (1853–1939) designed the Royal Sick Children's Hospital, Braid Church and his own house at No. 17 Blackford Road.

The 1930s style of architecture is also represented by Sir William Kininmonth's own house in Dick Place.

GRANGE CEMETERY

GRANGE CEMETERY was laid out on twelve acres of ground in 1847 by the Edinburgh Southern Cemetery Company Limited. The design, by the architect David Bryce, allowed for different categories of burial ground, a series of vaults in the centre, and a mortuary chapel. The intended opening of the cemetery was announced to shareholders and others in the *Edinburgh Courant* for 17th May 1845:

91

Edinburgh Southern Cemetery Company. Directors of the Company deem it to be their duty to inform the shareholders that the arrangements for commencing to lay out the Grounds at the Grange are in a forward state; the Plans for doing so, which are under the consideration of David Bryce, Esq., architect and C. C. Halket of Lawhill, being nearly completed.

A purchase of the property in Causewayside opposite Salisbury Place Newington through which the entrance to the Cemetery is to be made has been arranged and the operations will be immediately commenced for the formation of the Cemetery and its approaches.
16.5.1845

The first prospectus, in flowery Victorian style, appears to alternate between a sales document and a catalogue of endless expressions of sympathy. It opens with confirmation that the Grange would be able to provide every advantage in amenity, beauty of situation and proximity to the City. The main approach was by Grange Road but 'The Directors cherish the hope that ere long the centre walk of the Meadows may be opened to carriages for the accommodation of the Public . . .' With possible reference to the days of the resurrectionists, the prospectus claimed the 'highest attainable security that the remains therein deposited shall continue undisturbed'.

Costs were considered to be moderate and could be paid by instalments. In advocating a private burying ground for everyone, the prospectus stated that: 'Near this spot, weeping friends, after some afflicting bereavement, would often meet. Around it the associations of memory, at all times, would fondly play, and the affections of the heart tenderly cling'. The cost was between £2 and £12. The public ground was considerably cheaper, where the Directors felt compelled to announce a qualification to the ideal that 'remains . . . shall continue undisturbed'. No promise could be made that such a grave would never be disturbed in the future, but a guarantee was given that it would be undisturbed for at least ten years from the time of the first interment. Access to individual graves was greatly enhanced by broad walks or pathways and the Cemetery Company kept two hearses for hire 'so that the old and highly objectionable method of conducting Funerals by Spokes or on Shoulders may be superseded'.

A line of vaults was erected in the centre of the cemetery, partially hidden by a raised bank on either side. Bryce intended the high ground to be occupied by a Mortuary Chapel. The shareholders were against the idea, but they had no objection to a space being left for it in the future. As the space was never filled, it may be assumed that not only were Bryce's plans 'up in the air' but so too were the hands of the shareholders when the against-vote was taken. At the north-east cemetery gates, a house, designed by Bryce for the superintendent, was later extended to include another bay to the west, and a lean-to conservatory.

In January 1883 Grange Cemetery, along with those at Warriston, Echobank, Rosebank and Dean, was included in a Report by Henry J. Littlejohn, Medical Officer of Health for Edinburgh. Certain activities at Dalry Cemetery had come to his notice which suggested that all was not well at that burial ground. On receiving a letter from a citizen living near Dalry Cemetery, Littlejohn directed one of his inspectors to visit Dalry Cemetery in the company of the correspondent. They visited the cemetery at night on several occasions and discovered that some recent interments of children had been made very near to the surface. Further observation revealed a most unusual and macabre practice. Bodies of children recently interred were being exhumed and removed to nearby vaults where they were kept in secrecy until another body, usually that of an adult, was buried during a normal funeral in the child's grave. At night the grave was again opened and the body, which had been hidden in the vaults, was re-interred above the more recent corpse. In an endeavour to establish if the 'double burial' practice was widespread the inspectors made various measurements of the depth of graves. Of forty measurements taken in the common ground, the average depth was about two feet and the depth of the graves ranged from two feet to six inches from the surface. The otherwise impeccable language of the Report lapsed slightly in stating that the only qualification to the measurements was that they were taken at night and that 'their rigid accuracy cannot be depended on'. Nevertheless, there was a *prima facie* case to answer. Littlejohn brought the matter to the attention of the Public Health Committee and obtained its authority to conduct a public investigation, and to include all the cemeteries in the inquiry. Dalry was revisited and a further thirty borings were made of which only one was over three feet; the others ranged from eight inches below the surface to two feet eleven inches; and eleven were under two feet. The catacombs and vaults were also inspected but nothing unusual was found 'with the exception of an empty coffin'. The other cemeteries were also included. Grange Cemetery was visited on 12th April 1882 when one hundred and thirteen borings were made of which fifty-one were under three feet; seven were at three feet; and the lowest was one foot and eight inches.

Grange continued as a very popular and apparently well managed cemetery. In the early 1920s the Directors resolved to extend the burial ground westward towards Kilgraston Road. They acquired the houses Nos. 3 and 5 Kilgraston Road owned respectively by Joseph Bliss and Major Innocent and applied to the Dean of Guild Court in 'blissful innocence' to have them demolished. The gateways were blocked up and the boundary walls heightened and altered in order to bring the extension within the original cemetery ground. The plans were approved shortly after the architect T. Aikman Swan completed his drawings in July 1924. The entire cemetery came under the control of Edinburgh District Council in 1976 and has continued to be kept in good order, in stark contrast to many other Edinburgh burial grounds.

Unfortunately serious vandalism occurred in September 1977 when sixty-seven headstones were toppled. The incident highlighted the problem of protecting graves and the huge concentration of ornamental headstones, many of which are works of art by well-known sculptors of the day. To list all the famous persons interred and to describe the work of the various sculptors is an almost impossible task, but the Environmental Health Department has recently issued an Historical Fact Sheet giving a random selection, among which are the following:

SIR JAMES GOWANS b. 1821 — d. 1890
An unusual triangular headstone with stepped corbelled canopy.

WILLIAM STUART b. 1826 — d. 1868
A highly unusual monument in the form of an Egyptian temple flanked by two broken obelisks bearing the names of the interred. A large palm tree stands in the centre carved in bold relief.

REV THOMAS CHALMERS D.D., LL.D. b. 1780 — d. 1847
Professor of Moral Philosophy at St. Andrews and of Divinity at Edinburgh. First Moderator of the Free Church.

HUGH MILLER b. 1802 — d. 1856
Trained as a stonemason, later the country's leading authority on geology. Poet and author.

IVAN SZABO OF TRANSYLVANIA b. 1822 — d. 1858
Photographer. Grave marked by a small tower-like Gothic monument.

JAMES SMITH b. 1824 — d. 1887
Printer, poet and Scottish story writer. A bronze medallion head, by C. M. Bride, inset on large rugged red sandstone monument.

McCallum's monument c. 1935
A very pleasing monument with a full-size female figure leaning mournfully on the tablet, holding a small wreath in her left hand.

The Johnstones monument c. 1860
A twenty-feet high obelisk to the memory of Christian Johnstone, b. 1781 — d. 1857, authoress of *Edinburgh Tales* and other works and principal contributor to *Tait's Magazine*. Also her husband John Johnstone, b. 1779 — d. 1857, schoolmaster, editor of the *Inverness Courier*.

Sir Thomas Dick-Lauder b. 1784 — d. 1848
Owner of Grange House and estate, author of *The Wolfe of Badenoch* and other works.

Dr David Irving b. 1778 — d. 1860
Author and grammarian, keeper of Advocates' Library — insisted that the word was *Scotish* with one 't'.

John Hutchison R.S.A. b. 1832 — d. 1910
Sculptor whose work can be seen in Dean, Warriston, and Grange.

Thomas Usher, Brewer b. 1821 — d. 1896

Rev Thomas Guthrie b. 1803 — d. 1873
Preacher and philanthropist, Minister of Greyfriars before the Disruption of 1843, founder of Dr. Guthrie's School.

CARLTON CRICKET CLUB

IN 1832, SOME MEMBERS OF THE EDINBURGH SPECULATIVE SOCIETY, said to be bored by the evening's proceedings, fled from the debating chamber and formed a cricket club. They called it the Grange Cricket Club from the name of its first ground — a field lent by Sir Thomas Dick-Lauder of Grange.

The members did not stay long in the district, but used the name, Grange, at various locations in Edinburgh, before settling at Raeburn Place in 1872.

Meantime, the district of Grange did have a cricket club of its own, which also came into being in rather unusual circumstances. It was founded by a group of young men who had all been members of the Young Men's Christian Association, which had its meeting rooms in Adam Square. The Association had a Literary and Debating Society which held a Social Entertainment every year in Queen Street Hall. During the winter of 1862~1863 it was proposed to have a 'dramatic performance' by some of the members, who were to appear in costumes appropriate to the characters represented. The Association's Committee of Management was totally opposed to the idea, but the entertainment went ahead, and the four leaders were duly expelled. They formed a rival debating society to exercise their minds during the winter months, and also formed a cricket club for the summer: 'and the promoters, being very "Tory" named it the "Carlton Cricket Club" after the Carlton Club in London'.

During the first two seasons, matches were played in the Meadows, against various clubs, including the Royal High School and Edinburgh Caledonian. In 1866 the committee obtained permission to use a field 'directly opposite Grange House Lodge in Grange Loan', which was shared with the Edinburgh Caledonian Cricket Club until it was disbanded in 1868. However, the ground was never really satisfactory and in 1869 a move was made to Old Grange Loan ground to the south of Craigmount House Park. Even then the state of the cricket pitch was such that a sports report of 1871 observed that the Carlton v Dalkeith match was played 'on a wicket that was very bad, even for the Carlton ground, and was much complained of by both sides'. Carlton rose to the occasion in the following year, however, when they hosted a match between the United South of England XI and XXII Gentlemen of Edinburgh. The club obtained the use of a much better ground belonging to Mr Sime, the proprietor of

Craigmount Park, immediately to the north of the Old Grange Loan ground. An attendance of over three thousand spectators ensured a handsome profit of £100 for Carlton. A few years later it was hoped to repeat the success with a match against the Clown Cricketers, made up of professionals from the South of England. As Mr Sime's ground was not available, Carlton prepared the Old Grange Loan ground by employing Stratton the road contractors of Upper Grey Street. They put on their heaviest road roller, levelled the square to near perfection — and in the process smashed nearly every drain pipe under the turf.

In the early part of the twentieth century, Dr N. L. Stevenson, undoubtedly the major personality in the history of the club, and author of its history *Play*, set his heart on acquiring Grange Park as the new ground for the club. The Park, also on the north side of Grange Loan, was covered in trees and used to pasture cattle, but the proprietor, G. B. Thornton, was reluctant to enter into any agreement. After several attempts, Stevenson eventually obtained permission from Thornton, only to find that his committee did not back the proposal. Stevenson decided to go it alone, and arranged a Fancy Fair and Carnival which raised £1800 towards the cost of setting up the new ground. The trees were felled; the committee warmed to the idea of acquiring a new pitch; and after the dust and the turf had settled, the ground was opened on 17th May 1905. The move was reported in the *Scottish Referee* for April 1904:

> After being housed in what might be termed rather indifferent and unsuitable grounds since 1863, the Carlton have at last determined to flit and it is satisfactory to be able to state that their new ground at Grange Park, which is within a few minutes' walk of the old field is one of the finest in the district. The turf is hardly fit for this season's work, but by another year it should be in grand order.

In the years following the move to the new ground the club's fortunes varied considerably: 1912 was the fiftieth anniversary, but at the end of the First World War the ground was like a jungle, and the club was desperately short of good players. By 1922 the club had recovered from the temporary setback and celebrated the sixtieth anniversary, in style, at a dinner held in the North British Station Hotel. The following year brought further problems associated with the ground which was on a yearly lease. The proprietors were not keen to sell as they hoped to develop the ground with the 'adjacent mansionhouse', probably Grange Park (previously Egremont). In desperation the Carlton thought of bidding for the ground and the mansionhouse for future use as a school or a club. However, after considering the financial problems it was decided to put all resources into buying the ground only. A special committee was appointed on 1st June 1923 and almost exactly one year later the club was successful in buying the ground for the sum of £3,000.

During the latter years of the Second World War, Carlton's ground was used for military training, resulting in extensive damage to the pavilion and the ground where trenches were dug. In the immediate post-war period financial difficulties and a weaker playing team combined to create a low ebb, which did not change till the mid-1950s. The improvement in playing standards began with the arrival of the Rev. James Aitchison, one of Scotland's finest international players, who joined the club in 1954 and was followed, in subsequent years, by other good players. During the late 1950s and early 1960s the club's finances benefited greatly from a successful campaign to recruit more local members.

The centenary was celebrated in 1963 with a cricket week — almost ruined by bad weather — a dinner in the Carlton Hotel, and a lunch at the City Chambers hosted by the Lord Provost. The opportunity was also taken to replace the ageing club pavilion, probably dating from 1905, by a new structure formed from two 'prefab' houses no longer considered suitable as domestic residences. At the 125th anniversary in 1988 a cricket week was again held, and also an anniversary dinner. The club's steadily improving playing abilities secured the League Championship for the first time (after being runners-up on a number of occasions) and the local knock-out competition both in the anniversary year.

Whilst Dr N. L. Stevenson was certainly the outstanding figure in Carlton's history before the Second World War, three people have probably had the greatest influence on the club since then: James Jappy served Carlton from 1946 as player, secretary, umpire and president until his death in 1980; Mrs Margaret Masterton, patron and later Honorary President, made a number of financial donations to the club in addition to a substantial legacy on her death in 1988; and Alun Davies (the President), who joined the club in 1961, was a leading player for twenty-five years and Club Captain for thirteen successive seasons.

WHITEHOUSE AND GRANGE BOWLING CLUB

IN THE LATTER HALF OF THE NINETEENTH CENTURY the game of bowls was enjoying great popularity in Edinburgh, with new greens being opened at Trinity in 1855, Leith 1857, Lutton Place 1860, West End 1864, Summerside 1869 and Hillside 1870. As none of these greens was particularly near the districts of Grange, and Marchmont, a group of city business-men formed a committee on 5th January 1872 to search for a suitable site for a new club. Despite the initial euphoria, only fourteen people attended a meeting at the Southside Literary Institute in South Clerk Street to hear the committee's report on the proposed Whitehouse and Grange Bowling Club. The committee acquired a feu of ground in Hope Terrace extending to three-quarters of an acre from George Harrison (later Sir George, Lord Provost of Edinburgh), and set about considering the cost of forming the new club. The capital outlay to provide a clubhouse at £173 and to construct the green at £200 was financed by an ingenious system of issuing shares to would-be members. One thousand redeemable shares of £5 each were issued 'to be held entirely by members of the Club and to bear interest at the rate of 5% per annum'. Membership, at one guinea, was limited to seventy-five persons but the number of shares issued increased to one hundred and forty-seven, possibly on account of the remission of the annual subscription to holders of four or more shares.

The construction of the green was delayed by work being done for the cable-car system, which was routed along Hope Terrace and Clinton Road before Strathearn Place was opened up in 1899. The cost of the ground, clubhouse, green and implements was £855, and a greenkeeper was employed at £25 for six months. Membership rose to sixty with an additional membership of twenty-seven in 1873 and twenty-five in 1874, mostly made up of lawyers, bank managers, doctors, retired army personnel and ministers from the immediate area of Grange and Marchmont. The green was opened on 23rd May 1873 and in the same year a proposal was made to construct a curling pond on the extra ground to the south. The pond was created in 1874 with membership of the club limited to those who were already members of the bowling club, but a more controversial proposal, in 1875, to use the new area for roller skating, was firmly rejected. All these amenities had been organised by the original committee (which included George Harrison), led by the first President, W. R. Clapperton, and the first secretary, R. M. Russell.

By 1911 the club had been in existence for nearly forty years and it had a long waiting list. The extra membership, whilst welcome, was putting considerable pressure on the limited facilities available. Dr John Orr led a campaign to renew the clubhouse and to extend the green to the south. Although no action was taken on the green extension until 1922, the committee decided to engage the architect George Washington Browne to design a new clubhouse. Work went ahead almost immediately and the new building was opened

Whitehouse and Grange Bowling Club in Hope Terrace was founded in 1872 by a group of city businessmen who raised the capital by buying £5 shares in the club. Courtesy of Whitehouse and Grange Bowling Club.

in May 1912. The improved facilities were of great benefit, especially for home fixtures with various other clubs which included St. Ronans, Dunfermline and Dunbar. The first ladies' day was held in 1919.

In 1933 Dr Orr again raised the question of the clubhouse, suggesting that it should be demolished and a new one erected in a more suitable position. However there was general reluctance to demolish Browne's elevation and it was not until the 1960s that any large-scale alterations were carried out. Improvements were made to the south end of the building in 1965, and a much larger alteration in 1969 in anticipation of the centenary year. After the improvements were completed Associated Lady Members were admitted for the first time.

In May 1972 the club celebrated its centenary with a full

week of sporting and social events, concluding with a special church service on 28th May at what was then Grange Parish Church. A short history of the club, *Whitehouse and Grange Bowling Club 1872–1972*, was compiled from the records which have been kept meticulously since inception.

CHAPTER 6

CHURCHES

THE NUMBER AND VARIETY OF CHURCH BUILDINGS
established in and around Sciennes and the Grange owe
much to the different denominations which existed before
the great reunion of the Established Church in 1929. As the
population moved further south in the second half of the
nineteenth century each of the denominations was keen to
establish new churches in the neighbourhood. Many of these
had existing connections with much older churches in the
Old Town. Congregations raised substantial sums of money
to employ architects of the highest calibre to design and
superintend the construction of imposing buildings in
prominent locations.

In the second half of the twentieth century post-union
rationalisation, shortage of ministers, and movement of
population to new housing areas resulted in several unions
taking place between two, and sometimes three, separate
congregations. Some fine buildings were found to be surplus
to requirements: some were lost, whilst others were redeveloped for secular use. On the positive side, however,
many have survived in a much stronger position, supported
by a larger combined congregation.

Church histories appear to be almost a necessary part of
every congregation, usually written to mark the fiftieth or
hundredth anniversary, or at the time of a union with another
congregation. Valuable material is available from them,
particularly in connection with the real work of the church in
the neighbourhood and in foreign mission projects.

The architecture of all the churches is dealt with in
detail in *The Buildings of Scotland — Edinburgh*, and their

origins are described and traced with great accuracy in *The Kirks of Edinburgh* by the Rev. A. Ian Dunlop.

MARCHMONT ST. GILES CHURCH

MARCHMONT ST. GILES was formed in 1972 from the union of three other churches, namely West St. Giles, Grange and Warrender. After the union, West St. Giles building in Argyle Park Terrace was demolished and replaced by a block of flats for Viewpoint Housing Association, Warrender in Whitehouse Loan was converted to flats after remaining empty for some time, and Grange, in Kilgraston Road, was retained as the place of worship for the combined congregation. As a result of the union, Marchmont St. Giles retained the status of a burgh church in continuation of that ancient right previously held by West St. Giles, the oldest of the three congregations.

The date 1699 is usually taken as the origin of West St. Giles Church, being the year in which a congregation was established in Haddo's Hole in the north-west corner of St. Giles Cathedral. The city authorities provided accommodation in Haddo's Hole for people who had been worshipping in a 'meeting house in the Lawnmarket' since King James VII allowed toleration for Presbyterians as well as Roman Catholics. The name Haddo's Hole is derived from Sir John Gordon of Haddo who was imprisoned there before his execution in 1641. Under its subsequent name, New North Church, the congregation met in part of St. Giles until 1829 when it moved out to allow 'restoration' work to be done to the cathedral. They met first in the Methodist Church in Nicolson Square and then in Brighton Street Chapel. They returned to St. Giles as 'West St. Giles', using the western part of the cathedral building, but when Dr William Chambers wished to complete the unification of the cathedral as the place of worship of one congregation, arrangements were made for the congregation of West St. Giles to move out. At a meeting with the Kirk Session on 21st May 1879, it

105

was agreed that the congregation of West St. Giles would build a new church. With a gift of £10,000, an old detached villa, Meadow Lodge, at the west end of the recently built Argyle Park Terrace, was acquired for £2,400, and the architects, Hardy and Wight, were commissioned to draw up plans. The completed church, with a tall slender Gothic spire at its north-east corner, was opened on 17th January 1883. The church history is recorded in *The Story of West St. Giles Church 1699–1916.*

Warrender Church cannot claim the same antiquity as West St. Giles, being the youngest of the three congregations. It started life in November 1882 as Warrender Park Free Church as an offshoot of the Barclay Free Church, in response to a decision of the Free Church Presbytery to start a congregation in the developing district of Marchmont. To begin with, services were held in Viewpark School in Warrender Park Crescent but later a site on the west corner of Lauderdale Street and Warrender Park Road was secured on a five-year lease from Sir George Warrender. Plans were drawn by the architect, D. A. Robertson, for a temporary iron church which was erected in 1885. Two modest transepts were added in 1890. Shortly thereafter, the congregation took the decision to build a new stone church in Whitehouse Loan after considering several other sites. The foundation stone was laid on 23rd May 1891 by Professor A. R. Simpson M.D. and the church was opened on 2nd June 1892. The completed building, designed by R. M. Cameron in Italian Renaissance style, had a gallery round three sides, facing a raised, central pulpit with stairs on each side. Warrender Park Free Church became Warrender Park United Free in 1900 and Warrender in 1929. The jubilee history was written in *Warrender Church, Edinburgh 1886–1936.*

The third piece in the jigsaw is Grange Church. The earliest recorded meeting was on 21st November 1867 at No. 21 Findhorn Place when several residents of the Grange discussed the formation of a parish church in the district. In

West St. Giles Church at Meadow Place, 1973, shortly before its demolition. The congregation originated in the north-west corner of St. Giles Cathedral. Courtesy of the Royal Commission on the Ancient and Historical Monuments of Scotland.

January of the following year more definite plans were implemented and a fund was started for the construction of a stone church designed by the architect, Robert Morham. It was originally built as the Robertson Memorial Church in memory of the Rev. Dr James Robertson, Professor of Ecclesiastical History in the University of Edinburgh and Convenor of the Endowment Committee of the Church of Scotland, but from 1929 it was known as Grange Parish Church. Whilst the church was in the course of erection services were held in a small iron church which lay to the south of Beaufort Road. The church was opened on 1st October 1871 under its first minister, the Rev. W. L. Riach from Pencaitland.

The spire and clock of Robert Morham's church at the top of Kilgraston Road is undoubtedly one of the most prominent landmarks of south Edinburgh. Whilst the loss of the West St. Giles building was regrettable, it would have been even more disastrous to have lost such a fine example of Morham's work. The church lies east to west with the entrance doorway at the base of the huge west tower and spire, flanked by stair-halls to the north and south. On entering by the west door there is a feeling of spaciousness created by an extra hall, built in 1979, which is separated from the nave by a translucent screen wall. In the centre of the screen is a glass panel commemorating the union of the three churches in 1972, and on either side is a stained-glass panel brought from West St. Giles: to the left is St. Andrew and to the right the 1939-1945 War Memorial. At the south end of the hall are three windows presented by Charles Morton W.S., in August 1877, and at the north end are corresponding windows in memory of Janet Stirling Gowan, 1901. Below the Gowan window is the Esdaile oak bench, in memory of Helen P. Auld, headmistress of Esdaile in Kilgraston Road from 1918 to 1935. Beyond the screen the long nave opens into transepts to the north and south and culminates in a short apse. Reconstruction work undertaken in 1989 opened up the front of the church to provide more

The temporary Iron Church which was used by the congregation of the Robertson Memorial Church (now Marchmont St. Giles) in 1871. It lay between the present church and Beaufort Road.

space for special services, weddings and baptisms. A single gallery is located above the entrance hall.

The nave, apse and gallery are all lit by stained-glass windows, many of them by Ballantine and Gardiner, and provided by members of the congregation. These include: in the north wall of the nave two windows to the memory of the architect Robert Morham and his wife Janet Aird; in the north transept, windows in memory of Jane Barbour, wife of William Elliot Turnbull, 1902 and Barbara, wife of William James Turnbull; left of the apse a memorial to the Very Rev. David Paul D.D., LL.D., F.L.S., minister of the parish 1896 to 1919, Moderator of the General Assembly 1915; in the centre of the apse a twin window erected by Dr and Mrs John Orr in 1949; in the south transept two windows presented by A. B. Armitage, Church Treasurer 1893; and finally, in the south wall of the nave, two windows presented by Mrs McDowall in 1878. The south transept was converted into a side chapel in 1965 in memory of Mrs Helen Donaldson. It contains a communion table and a mosaic mural by Rae Howard Jones in memory of Elfrida Tindal, wife of the Rev. Professor William S. Tindal, Professor of Practical Theology at New College and an elder of Grange Church.

At the centenary in 1971 a canister, to be opened in the year 2071, was placed under the vestibule floor after the morning service on 21st November. It contained a copy of *The Scotsman*, *The Evening News*, *Life and Work*, coins of the Realm, a message from the congregation, and a letter from Mrs Margaret Pearson dated 1st October 1971:

> Dear Mr Finlayson
>
> I was interested to see in the *Evening News* today that you are celebrating the Centenary of the Robertson Memorial Church on Sunday. I do not think there can be anyone who remembers it earlier than I do. I was born in Great King Street in September 1873 and in 1878 my parents moved to Strathearn Place. They joined the Grange where Mr Riach was then minister and I used to go to church with them. I can still see in my mind's eye a door which had a curtain because of the draught. The curtain used to move with the draught and made some slight noise and I thought there was a lion behind it! Mr Riach had a very loud voice which my father did not like and we soon moved to Morningside Parish Church. In the 90's, I forget the year, my father's brother, David Paul, D.D., LL.D., became minister of the Grange. He was Moderator of the Church in 1915. My husband, the late Dr C. M. Pearson, was doctor to the Ministers' Daughters' College (Esdaile) for many years.
>
> Please accept my good wishes.
>
> Yours sincerely
>
> *Margaret M. Pearson*

REID MEMORIAL CHURCH

THE REID MEMORIAL CHURCH stands on the corner of West Savile Terrace and Blackford Avenue, its traditional east-west axis ensuring a magnificent view of its deeply recessed west window from Charterhall Road. The church, described in *The Buildings of Scotland: Edinburgh* as 'Lorimerian Gothic', was designed by Leslie G. Thomson and constructed, between 1929 and 1933, of Craigmillar stone, with Doddington dressings, and ironwork by Thomas Hadden. The stained-glass in the east windows of the chancel was the work of James Ballantine F.S.A. Scot., and the numerous sculptures were executed by Alexander Carrick, R.S.A.

Although the church celebrated its Golden Jubilee as recently as 1985, its origins go back to the middle of the nineteenth century in the Old Town of Edinburgh. At the time of the Disruption in 1843, many members of the congregation of the High Church (St. Giles), led by their minister the Rev. Dr Robert Gordon, joined the Free Church and formed the Free High Church. The problem of finding accommodation for the breakaway church was solved, firstly, by using the Music Hall in George Street. A more permanent home, however, was built at the head of the Mound, as part of the New College group, from designs by the architect David Bryce, who later undertook a major reconstruction of the Bank of Scotland building nearby. The congregation worshipped at the Mound until 31st December 1934 when about two hundred members elected to transfer to the new Reid Memorial Church, leaving the old church to be restored as New College Library. The new church was dedicated on 3rd January 1935 and the first service was held on 6th January.

Reid Memorial Church is of considerable architectural merit, and is described by the architect Leslie G. Thomson in his introductory booklet *The Reid Memorial Church*. This original description was augmented and extended in particular detail by Malcolm Anderson in *The Reid Memorial Church, Edinburgh — A Jubilee Description 1935-1985*. Mr Anderson,

111

an architect by profession and a member of the Kirk Session, is now the only member of Reid Memorial Church who transferred from the High Church. His deep interest in the church, and that of his family before him, is evident in his sympathetic interpretation of the many plaques and carvings throughout the building. The overall concept of the building is, however, evident from Mr Thomson's own words:

> In the general design, the principal aim was to secure, without unnecessary ornament, that Cathedral-like dignity which is ensured only by a lofty proportion, by that feeling of height and aspiration which indicates the theme running throughout the whole building, namely, that of the Ascension.

Externally the layout of the church is relatively simple. The lofty chancel at the east end is lit by three magnificent stained-glass windows, and the vestibule and main doorway are positioned at the west end. The nave, with shallow transepts to the north and south, is flanked by low aisles, which accentuate the height of the supporting buttresses and intervening windows. A tall, square, buttressed and lightly castellated tower dominates the north-east corner, completely dwarfing the much smaller tower with the ogee copper dome to the south. Externally, sculpture by Alexander Carrick is much in evidence. Several angels, each playing a different instrument (one on primitive bagpipes with short drones), adorn the head of the buttresses, and below the east window is a panel over a stone basin, depicting 'The Women at the Well of Samaria'. The main door, at the west end, lies within a low segmental archway, above which is the deeply recessed west window in leaded glass with purplish hues. The doorway is purposely uneventful, leading in Mr Anderson's words to the 'shadowed cavelike porch, and proceeds into a brilliant cathedral-like interior'.

Internally the lofty design is immediately apparent from the arrangement of the high windows and barrel-vaulted ceiling. The shallow transepts, in similar style, break to the

The public clock and spire of Marchmont St. Giles Church by the architect Robert Morham. It was opened as the Robertson Memorial Church on 1st October 1871. Photograph by Phyllis M. Cant.

left and to the right, leaving the central vista of the chancel unchallenged. The chancel has a high vaulted ceiling, richly embellished, and is lit by the three main sections of the east window: on the left is the Nativity; on the right is the Crucifixion; and in the centre, the Ascension. Below the east window, forming a backcloth to the stone communion table, is a picture of *The Last Supper* by William R. Lawson. The pulpit and lectern are also in stone, and all the doors, facings, choir stalls and elders' stalls are in oak, with numerous carvings.

The two most important inscriptions, which between them explain the history of Reid Memorial Church, are located in the transepts. In the south transept a bronze plaque, framed in oak, records the founding of the congregation in 1843, its transfer from the Mound in 1935, and the names of the ministers of the Free High Church. In the Jubilee account of the church a most apt acronym is highlighted from the surnames of these ministers, namely, Gordon, Rainy, Arnot, Smith and Simpson. When added to the slighty re-arranged surname *Robertson* — the first transferred minister — the six names form the GRASS ROOTS of the church from the time of the Disruption in 1843.

The second plaque is the intriguing memorial inscription to William Reid in the north transept:

TO THE GLORY OF GOD AND IN MEMORY OF
WILLIAM REID WAS THIS CHURCH BUILT,
IN THE YEARS 1929 to 1933 IN ACCORDANCE
WITH HIS LAST WISH, BY HIS SON, WILLIAM
CRAMBE REID WHO DEPARTED THIS LIFE
23RD DECEMBER 1921

Close examination of the lettering against the red background reveals that two words have been altered from the version which appears in Leslie G. Thomson's own description. Originally it read '. . . in accordance with *the* last wish *of* his son . . .'. The alteration is explained in a letter from the architect to the Session Clerk producing evidence from the wife of one of the Trustees (Mrs Smith, a niece of the late William Crambe Reid) that it was William Crambe Reid's father who had expressed the wish to have the church built.

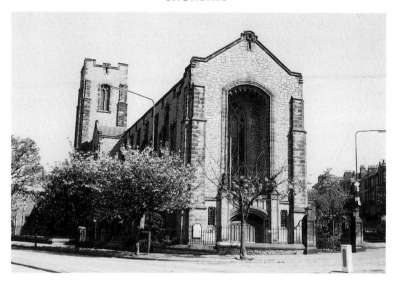

Reid Memorial Church, designed by Leslie G. Thomson in 'Lorimerian Gothic' and constructed between 1929 and 1933 of Craigmillar stone. Photograph by Phyllis M. Cant.

William Reid, a successful Edinburgh businessman, was a prominent member of Free St. John's Church, and set up a number of charitable trusts, some of which are still operating.

The ancillary church buildings are all grouped around the Cloister Courtyard to the east of the main building. The courtyard dates from the same time as the church and consists of a grass and paved square, enclosed by the vestries on the west side, the original church hall on the south side, a loggia on the east side, and the church officer's house, screen wall and session room on the north side. The architecture and stonework throughout are in keeping with the remainder of the church and there are numerous examples of Thomas Hadden's ironwork, including a small rostrum projecting from the loggia. Immediately opposite the loggia, on the west side of the courtyard, is Alexander Carrick's relief panel of 'The Women at the Well of Samaria'. A new church hall, entered from the loggia, was constructed to the south-east of the courtyard in 1961, and the old hall has been converted

115

E

to a suite of function rooms as a memorial to the Rev. Ian M. Macgregor, minister of the parish from 1954 to 1984. Mr Macgregor was succeeded in 1985 by the present minister, the Rev. B. M. Embleton.

The Reid Memorial Church celebrated its fifty-year jubilee in 1985 with a commemorative service on 6th January, and an exhibition of memorabilia of the High Church and of the Reid. A fête was held in the Cloister Courtyard and church halls on 8th June 1985 which raised £1,650 for three local charities, St. Crispin's School for Handicapped Children (to which the minister of the Reid has been chaplain since it was opened in 1963), the Royal Scottish Society for the Prevention of Cruelty to Children, and the Madame Curie Hospice.

St. Catherine's – Argyle Church

St. Catherine's–Argyle, on the corner of Grange Road and Chalmers Crescent, was formed in 1968 from the union of two local churches, namely Argyle Place and St. Catherine's in Grange. Both churches had a distinctive history prior to the formation of the combined congregation.

Argyle Place United Presbyterian Church was the younger of the two churches. Its congregation was formed on 3rd April 1877 primarily from persons 'favourable to the formation of a church in Edinburgh on temperance principles', who had objected to the use of fermented wine at Communion. The first service was taken by the Rev. James Robertson Jnr., on 13th May 1877, and a site for a new church building was acquired on the corner of Sciennes Road and Chalmers Crescent. Plans were drawn by the architects, Alexander McTavish, and the foundation stone was laid on 1st November 1879 by Lord Provost William Collins of Glasgow. The completed building, enhanced by a tall slender spire of grey stone, cost just over £6,000 and seated nine hundred people. Argyle Place United Presbyterian

Edinburgh Area Scout Pipe Band in West Saville Terrace prior to the opening of the Reid Memorial Church Jubilee Fête in 1985. Photograph by Robin Cavaye.

Church became Argyle Place United Free Church in 1900 and then Argyle Place Church in 1929. In the Basis for Union with St. Catherine's in Grange in 1968, it was agreed that the Argyle Place building would be the place of worship and plans were made to convert St. Catherine's in Grange to hall accommodation. After substantial sums of money had been expended, the Argyle Place church building was extensively damaged by fire in 1974, resulting in its demolition shortly thereafter. The Grange Road building was again altered to a place of worship and reconsecrated on 23rd September 1979 at a service presided over by the Very Rev. Dr R. Leonard Small.

The story of St. Catherine's in Grange is older than that of Argyle Place Church. It started life as a Free Church around 1861 when a group of members from Roxburgh Free Church met in a hall in Causewayside. They were later joined by another group who attended services in 1863 conducted by the Rev. Professor Smeaton D.D., in his dining room at No. 13 (now 37) Mansionhouse Road. In 1865 a new congregation was formed, a site was secured on the corner of Grange Road and Chalmers Crescent and the foundation stone for the new church was laid by Lord Kintore on 13th October 1865. The original intention was to take a larger feu of ground stretching from Mansionhouse Road (North) to Chalmers Crescent, and to close up Lovers' Loan which ran between the west part of the feu, intended for the church building, and the east part which was intended for the manse. However, when the City authorities refused to allow the alteration to Lovers' Loan the congregation abandoned the idea of building the manse adjacent to the church. The T-shaped church building, designed by Patrick Wilson, was built of grey stone with several pink granite shafts, principally around the south-facing entrance. An octagonal belfry was constructed to the west of the entrance but lack of funds prevented completion of the steeple to the east. The problem of the unfinished steeple was considered again in 1875 when a full meeting of the Deacons' Court unanimously resolved to have the work done. A committee was formed to put the work in hand, estimated by the architect, Mr Wilson, to cost £2,200. Members of the congregation were invited to make subscriptions over a period of two or three years from 11th November 1875, but although a substantial sum was received, it was insufficient for the purpose.

When the church was first opened on 6th December 1866 it was officially named Chalmers Memorial Free Church, but under its first minister, the Rev. Dr Horatius Bonar, it was generally known as the Grange Free Church. Horatius Bonar was born in 1808 at Old Broughton in Edinburgh, the sixth son of James Bonar, the Search Solicitor of Excise for Scotland, and his wife Marjory Maitland. He was educated at the High School, Edinburgh University and Divinity Hall, after which he was licensed to preach by the Presbytery of Edinburgh on 27th April 1833. He was assistant at South Leith Parish Church for four years before obtaining

St. Catherine's Argyle Church in Grange Road which opened on 6th December 1866 as Chalmers Memorial Free Church under its first minister, the Rev. Dr Horatius Bonar, the great hymn writer.

his first charge at North Church, Kelso, on 30th November 1837. At the Disruption in 1843 Bonar was one of only three ministers in the Kelso Presbytery who 'came out' in support of the Free Church. Bonar remained at Kelso until 1866 when he accepted the challenge of the new Free church in the heart of the Grange, appropriately named the Chalmers Memorial Free Church, where he remained until 1889. In addition to his pastoral duties, Bonar was a prolific writer. He wrote several books, over six hundred hymns and poems, and countless evangelical tracts, most of which were reprinted on several occasions: *God's Way of Peace* had a circulation of 285,000 copies; *The Night of Weeping* 59,000; and *Hymn of Faith and Hope* 150,000. His most famous tract was *Believe and Live* of which a million copies were produced. In 1883 Bonar, at the age of seventy-five, was elected Moderator of the Free Church of Scotland, but the additional responsibilities began to tell on his health and on 11th September

1887 he preached his last sermon at the Grange. He died on 31st July 1889 and was buried at Canongate Churchyard. The centenary of his death was commemorated by St. Catherine's—Argyle Church with a small exhibition of memorabilia connected with Horatius Bonar, a service of praise using some of his hymns, and the publication of a most informative booklet, *Horatius Bonar and His Hymns*, by Graham L. Gibb.

Chalmers Memorial Free Church, or Grange Free Church, has changed its name on several occasions: in 1900 it was renamed Grange United Free Church; in 1929 it became St. Catherine's in Grange; and in 1968, on the union with Argyle Place Church, it adopted its present title St. Catherine's—Argyle. Although the exterior of Patrick Wilson's original church remains almost intact, the interior has been greatly altered. The original layout probably ends at the vestibule with the life-size medallion portrait of Bonar, in Sicilian marble, by the sculptor George J. Webster, 1890. In the main body of the church a much lower suspended ceiling now masks the huge roof timbers, galleries and stained-glass windows. The original north-south axis of pulpit and pews has been re-orientated so that the modern seating, for four hundred faces east towards a broad, shallow chancel with the pulpit in the north-east corner. The pulpit is not the original, having been brought from St. Margaret's, Juniper Green when St. Catherine's—Argyle was reconstructed in 1979. The organ was salvaged from Argyle Place Church and rebuilt in what was the south gallery. Externally the alterations are minimal and in keeping with the remainder of the building. A small vestry was demolished and replaced in 1982 by an extension on the east side accommodating a new vestry and several committee and general-purpose rooms.

Perhaps the most intriguing link with the untimely demise of Argyle Place Church is the pulpit fall. It was rescued from the debris of the fire in 1974 and painstakingly restored by Mrs. L. Kindberg of Chester Street. The bold central cross, against an azure background, is now flanked by intricate needlework depicting engulfing flames, held in check by the words NEC TAMEN CONSUMEBATUR (AND YET WAS NOT CONSUMED).

A comprehensive account of the history of the church is contained in *St. Catherine's in Grange Church – A Centenary History 1866–1966*.

SALISBURY CHURCH

SALISBURY CHURCH, on the corner of Grange Road and Causewayside, was formed in 1940 under its previous name Newington South and Hope Park. It took the name Salisbury in 1958. The 1940 union brought together the separate congregations of Newington South Church (in the Salisbury building) and Hope Park Church which stood on the south-east corner of Hope Park Terrace and Summerhall.

The Hope Park congregation was formed on 2nd May 1792 by secession from Crosscauseway. The secessionists met in Lady Lawson Wynd and then built a permanent church in Potterrow, which was opened in 1793. However, further division was inevitable when the minister, the Rev. Thomas McCrie, took an active part in forming the 'Constitutional Presbytery of Whitburn'. The congregation divided, the majority following McCrie to Carrubber's Close and then to a new church on the corner of West Richmond Street and Davie Street.

The Potterrow United Presbyterian congregation built a new church at Summerhall, costing £6700 and seating over one thousand, which was opened by Dr Cairns of Berwick on 16th September 1867. The Summerhall building was a very distinctive landmark for many years before its demolition for an extension to the Royal Dick Veterinary College. It lay on an east-west axis, the west-facing doorway surmounted by a pedimented overdoor and wheel window. The north and south transepts were triple-gabled with a stone cross on each apex, and wheel windows in the clerestory. The most prominent feature was the square bell tower and spire on the north-west corner, built in one rise for over half its height. The upper part of the tower had louvred lights above which were hooded pediments supporting a short stubby stone spire.

Over the years the congregation changed its name on several occasions. Potterrow Antiburgher became Potterrow United Associate Secession in 1820, Potterrow United Presbyterian in 1847, Hope Park United Presbyterian in 1867, Hope Park United Free in 1900, Hope Park in 1929 and so to the union in 1940.

The congregation of Newington South owes its existence to the initiative of three young men, Robert Paterson, James Middlemass and Andrew Taylor, members of the United Presbyterian Church. In 1847 they saw the opportunity of buying Duncan Street Chapel which was in the process of being sold by the Baptists. After discussing the matter with the Presbytery and other sympathisers, an offer of £1200 was put in and accepted. The first service was conducted on 9th January 1848 by Dr Brown of Broughton Place. In the first year a Missionary Association was founded, employing a full-time missionary at a salary of £50 per annum 'to labour in Causewayside'. Of all the people to hold the appointment, perhaps the most inspirational was James Goodfellow whose forty years' experience in the district is recorded in his book, *The Print of His Shoe*, published in 1906, which is of interest both for its information on tragic case histories and the general topographical descriptions of the district in the latter part of the nineteenth century.

By the early 1860s the Duncan Street building was insufficient for the increased congregation and a fund was started to build a new church. A committee was appointed to look for a site suitable for the districts of Newington, Causewayside and Grange, the recommendation being the north corner of Grange Road and Causewayside. The architect, Robert Paterson, was asked to draw plans for a

Hope Park United Free Church stood on the corner of Hope Park Terrace and Summerhall until it was demolished to make way for a modern extension to the Royal Dick Veterinary College.

church to seat one thousand, within a budget of £6000, which eventually rose to £6761. The completed church was opened on 15th November 1863. Although the congregation grew steadily, there were two occasions when fairly substantial numbers were lost. The first was in October 1873 when several members seceded over the question of using unfermented wine at communion. The dissenters left to join others from Lothian Road Church in the formation of Argyle Place Church. The second occasion was in 1877, under somewhat happier circumstances, when some of the congregation moved to establish the new Rosehall United Presbyterian Church in Dalkeith Road.

Newington South has not experienced quite so many changes of name as its partner Hope Park. Duncan Street United Presbyterian became Grange Road United Presbyterian in 1863, Newington South United Free in 1900, and Newington South in 1929. At least two histories of the church have been written, namely *Newington United Presbyterian Church Jubilee Memorial 1848–1898* and *A Brief History of Newington South Church 1848–1948*.

Salisbury Church was designed by Robert Paterson in 1862. It is a chunky, two-storey building with a short square tower on its south-east corner. Its lucarned pavilion roof has lost its original ironwork, giving the short belfry a somewhat truncated appearance. Entry from the east doorway leads to a spacious vestibule with stairs to the gallery on the north and south side. The vestibule has a relief carving of the Rev. James Robertson, the first minister in 1848, below which are the War Memorials. The south wall displays a small pedimented stone, with Hebrew lettering and the date 1792, which was brought from Hope Park Church and before that formed part of the building at Potterrow. The nave is brightly decorated with a deeply corniced roof, and side seating under the gallery which extends round three sides of the church. The east gallery is steeply raked from the clock to the large wheel window at the rear. There is no chancel, as such, but the pulpit is positioned at the west end with the organ pipes behind it and the organ to the north. The original water-powered organ, dating from 1883, cost £1065 to purchase and instal.

The clerestory is lit by several pairs of windows but they are not of stained-glass. In the south wall of the nave is the stained-glass Taylor Memorial and two similar windows to members of the Baxter family. The centre window in the north wall of the nave is a memorial to those members of the congregation who were killed in the First World War.

MAYFIELD CHURCH

MAYFIELD CHURCH congregation was formed in 1958 from the union of Mayfield North Church and Fountainhall Road Church. At the time of the union the congregation was known by the combined name of Mayfield and Fountainhall, but in 1968 the name was simplified to Mayfield. The distinctive building with the spire and clock, at the corner of West Mayfield and Mayfield Road, was adopted as the new place of worship. Before the union, both churches, Mayfield North and Fountainhall Road, had quite distinct histories which have been recorded on numerous occasions in the past.

The Fountainhall Road history is the older of the two. It dates from 1828 when the congregation was formed from the secession of a group from Bristo United Secession Church. They met firstly in Bethel Chapel in the High Street, and then in the Freemasons' Hall, before taking the ambitious step of buying a large chapel in the Cowgate which had been acquired from the Episcopalians in 1818 for a Relief Congregation. As there was seating for two thousand, it was eventually realised that the plan had been too ambitious and the building was sold in 1856, and became St. Patrick's Roman Catholic Church. The congregation moved to more modest premises in Infirmary Street where they remained until a new church was built in 1897 on the south side of Fountainhall Road. This church, under the name Mayfield United Presbyterian, became Fountainhall Road United Free in 1900 and Fountainhall Road in 1929. When the Reid Memorial Church was under construction the suggestion was put to, and approved by, the congregation that they would move to the new building in West Savile Terrace, but the General Assembly refused to endorse the proposal. A somewhat disappointed congregation was also affected by the absence of its minister, the Rev. Magnus Nicolson, for long periods during the Second World War. By 1955 the congregation was just over two hundred, making it hardly sustainable as a full charge. When Mr Nicolson transferred to Banffshire in 1956 the opportunity was taken to propose the union with Mayfield North. After the union, the Fountainhall Road building, designed by Graham Fairley, was sold to Work and Witness, an interdenominational body, formed to develop the lay forces of the Scottish Churches. The centenary story of Fountainhall Road Church was written very comprehensively by J. J. Walker in *Fountainhall Road Church Edinburgh, History of the Congregation 1828–1928*.

The history of Mayfield North can be traced to 1875 when the district to the south of West Mayfield was becoming more populous. The possibility of building a Free Church in the area had received considerable support, mainly through the initiative of Rev. Professor Blaikie of Free New North Church. Following a public meeting of interested persons, held on 13th March 1875 at Clare Hall, 18 Minto Street, a preaching station was formed called Mayfield Free Church. Services were held at Clare Hall until a permanent site for a new church was secured on the corner of West Mayfield and St. Andrew's Terrace (now part of Mayfield Road). Plans submitted by Hippolyte Blanc were accepted in January 1876 and a start was made, almost immediately, on the church hall which was opened on 3rd December 1876. The first minister was the Rev. J. T. Stuart of Kelso. The commemorative stone for the main church was laid by Lord

The tall elegant spire of Mayfield Church, designed by Hippolyte Blanc, and opened on 3rd December 1876. The bell, cast by John Taylor & Co. of Loughborough, was added in 1895. Photograph by Phyllis M. Cant.

Provost Sir Thomas Boyd on 5th October 1878, by which time much of the construction was underway. The church opened on 30th May 1879. The spire, clock and bell were added later with the help of a gift of £1000 from Mr Johnston Stewart. Mayfield Free became Mayfield United Free in 1900, Mayfield North in 1929, and so to the union with Fountainhall in 1958.

After the union, the building at West Mayfield was used for worship. In 1968 the adjacent church hall was greatly extended, and a large entrance hall was built between the church and church house to the east. All work was completed by October 1968 at a total cost of nearly £30,000. Little did the congregation know that their new accommodation would soon be urgently needed. On 11th January 1969 the roof of the church was extensively damaged by fire, necessitating lengthy and costly repair work, during which time services were held in the new hall. The opportunity was also taken to make some modifications to the layout, details of which are best appreciated in relation to Blanc's original plans.

The church, in French Gothic, is considered to be one of Blanc's finest buildings. It is constructed with the vestibule and entrance to the west, with a long nave leading into a short five-sided apse at the east end. The transepts to the north and south are double-gabled but the most prominent external feature is the square clock tower to which was added, in 1894, the stone spire with shafted pinnacles on each corner. The mechanics of the clock tower are worth close examination, despite the rather awkward access. The clock mechanism is housed on the floor below the clock faces. Before 1989, when the motive power was changed to electricity, the clock needed to be wound by hand each week, fifty-four revolutions each being required to raise the two weights from ground level. The power from the clock mechanism is relayed to the floor above by a system of spindles, which branch three ways to move the hands of each of the three clock faces: north, east and west. During the hours of darkness the faces were originally lit by gaslight, but although electricity was installed many years ago, the clock still relies on an ingenious variable wheel and arc to alter the switching-on time as the year progresses. Above the clock faces, on a heavily reinforced floor, is the great bell, also now operated by electricity. The chime is automatically cut out between 11 p.m. and 6.00 a.m. and can be adjusted manually for other occasions. The bell carries the inscription:

JOHN TAYLOR AND CO
FOUNDERS, LOUGHBOROUGH
MAYFIELD FREE CHURCH
LEWIS DAVIDSON M.A. MINISTER
1895

Internally the gallery is positioned over the vestibule, and the nave is separated from the aisles and transepts by a stone arcade. After the fire in 1969 the choir seating and the organ were removed to the gallery and the floor of the apse was extended at the same level, into the nave. The vestibule was also enlarged by the removal of some pews at the rear of the church. The high, round-arched, timber roof, which had been badly damaged, was replaced by a reticulated vault in white plaster. The pulpit was retained on the north side of the apse although its original position was in the centre. A simple cross, made by Ian Dodds, of timber from the fire-damaged roof, used during services in the hall, has been retained on a side communion table. The modern baptismal font has a pewter bowl with the inscription 'Cowgate Chapel 1818'. Fortunately, the extensive stained-glass work was not damaged in the fire.

The history of Mayfield Church has been written in at least three separate books: *Mayfield United Free Church 1875-1925* at the fiftieth anniversary; *Mayfield and Fountainhall*, a few years after the 1958 union; and *Mayfield 100* covering the years 1875 to 1975. Whenever the next account of the church is undertaken it will, no doubt, include the latest chapter in the history of Mayfield: in 1989 the minister, the Rev. W. J. G. McDonald, D.D., was appointed Moderator of the General Assembly of the Church of Scotland.

GERMAN LUTHERAN CHURCH

THE GERMAN LUTHERAN CONGREGATION came to Chalmers Crescent in 1954 to a site immediately opposite Argyle Place Church, which has since been demolished. However, the congregation can trace its history in Edinburgh to 1862 when Johann Blumenreich, with the assistance of the United Presbyterian Church and the Church of Scotland, obtained the use of a hall in Upper Queen Street for regular services. The hall was part of the United Presbyterian College, the remains of which survived until recently at the rear of the B.B.C. offices in Queen Street. The German congregation remained at Queen Street until 1879 when they built their own church, designed by James B. Wemyss, at the corner of Cornwallis Place and Rodney Street. At the outbreak of the First World War, as the congregation was unable to meet, it was disbanded and the church building was taken over by the Brethren. The congregation did not reconvene until after the end of the Second World War when temporary accommodation was obtained at St. Mary's Cathedral and Holy Trinity near Dean Bridge.

In the early 1950s No. 1 Chalmers Crescent was occupied by the Glendinning School of Dancing, but when it was discontinued, the premises were bought by the German Church. The old villa was used as a manse and the dance hall was converted to a place of worship. The congregation used the premises until 1966 when the original villa and dance hall were demolished and replaced by a new church, designed by Alfred Schilt of Frankfurt, and supervised by Alan Reiach & Partners of Edinburgh. The completed building, with a long stained-glass window of modern, abstract design by George Garson, includes the church, manse, hall, offices and a small library.

The congregation is drawn from the German community in Edinburgh and the East of Scotland, and the service is a mixture of the rites of the Lutheran and Presbyterian Churches.

130

CHAPTER 7

SCHOOLS

AS THE POPULATION OF SCIENNES AND THE GRANGE begin to increase in the middle of the nineteenth century, so did the number and variety of schools in the area. Many of these were small privately run establishments, usually owned by an experienced female principal who frequently operated from her own house. Detailed records for many of these schools have long since disappeared but sufficient information is available to provide some idea of the circumstances which gave rise to their foundation. In addition to the small private schools other larger institutions survived well into the twentieth century. By far the largest — but not the oldest — is Sciennes Primary School which will celebrate its centenary in 1992.

THE BELL ACADEMY

THE PEDIMENTED LINTEL STONE above the gateway to No. 15 Lauder Road carries the date, 1852, and the name of the house, St. Andrews Cottage. This imposing detached house was occupied for many years as 'a boarding and day school for young ladies' run by the Misses Maggie and Jessie Bell. The intriguing, but elusive, link between the Misses Bell of Lauder Road and Dr Andrew Bell's Madras College in St. Andrews has not yet been found, despite various researches over the last decade.

John Baron Bell began his Edinburgh teaching career in 1831 at No. 116 Rose Street. In the following year he moved to new premises at No. 3 St. Cuthbert Street, which ran westwards from Lothian Road across what is now the south side of Festival Square. When that part of the city was being redeveloped in 1838 he acquired more prestigious premises at No. 36 George Street, where he was in partnership for a short while with a Mr Pryde. Unfortunately, no definite connection has been established between John Baron Bell and James Bell of Dr Bell's School, who taught at Greenside from 1840 to 1845. By 1845 the partnership between Bell and Pryde had been dissolved and John Baron Bell was advertising his school in the following terms:

COMMERCIAL ACADEMY
36 George Street

Term Days — *1st Oct., 15th Dec., 1st March, 15th May.*

Mr J. B. Bell's Terms per 2½ Months			s.	d.
Writing, Arithmetic or Book-keeping 1 hour a day			10	—
″ ″ ″ 2 hours a day			15	—
″ ″ ″ 3 hours a day			18	—
″ ″ ″ 4 hours a day			21	—

Public Class Hours

From 1st Oct. to 1st March — from 9 a.m. to 1 p.m., and from 2 to 5 p.m.
From 1st March to 1st August — from 7 to 9 a.m., 10 a.m. to 1 p.m., and from 2 to 4 p.m.

Private Hours

Mr Bell receives Pupils daily after 5 o'clock p.m., and on Saturdays after 9 a.m., at his residence, 1, Darnaway Street.

Terms per Course of Twelve Lessons

One Pupil	£1	1	0
Two Pupils	1	11	6
Three Pupils	2	2	0

During his early teaching career J. B. Bell changed his private address on numerous occasions, but in 1852 he bought No. 15 Lauder Road, where he came to live with his wife and family. He maintained the Commercial Academy in George Street until his death in 1861. In the same year, the Misses Maggie and Jessie Bell (daughters of J. B. Bell) began to

A group of children at Bell Academy in Lauder Road, c. 1906, with Miss Maggie Bell in the centre. Courtesy of Dr James Gray.

advertise their school for young ladies at No. 15 Lauder Road, although it is possible that they were in business on a smaller scale for a few years prior to that date. Mrs Bell died in 1865 but James Adam Bell, a brother of Maggie and Jessie, lived at No. 15 from 1867 until his death in 1907. When Miss Jessie died in 1913 the school was continued by the surviving member of the family, Miss Maggie, until 1922. On her death No. 15 Lauder Road was sold to Miss Catherine Frances Mary McDonald.

Recollections of the school at Lauder Road around the turn of the century were recorded by Dr James Gray from Miss Margaret (Daisy) Buchanan of No. 13 Lauder Road, who died in 1988 at the age of ninety-seven. Miss Buchanan was the last surviving daughter of James Buchanan, the chemist of Oswald House, and a niece of Robert Morham, architect of the Robertson Memorial Church (now Marchmont St. Giles). She attended the Bell Academy from 1896 to

1901 before going on to Craigmount in Dick Place. The average number of pupils was somewhere between twenty and thirty, mostly ranging from age five to ten years, although a few remained until they were twelve. The subjects taught were writing, arithmetic, spelling, grammar, gymnastics, singing, and, for the older pupils, French. The social graces were encouraged under the maxim: 'the sign of a lady is a hat and a clean handkerchief'. No homework was given, either to the day pupils or the boarders. Encouragement, or discipline, was maintained by a simple system of reward or punishment which tended to be identified with one or other of the two Misses Bell. Miss Jessie administered corporal punishment, whilst Miss Maggie handed out sugar lumps. Such a system would have attracted a great deal of criticism from modern educationalists, but a sound basic education was obtained, and the recollections do relate to the closing years of the nineteenth century.

The Bell family maintained an unbroken commitment to education in Edinburgh for nearly a century, from 1831 to 1922. The family name, the strong teaching tradition and the name of the house, St. Andrews Cottage, all suggest some connection with Dr Andrew Bell of Madras College in St. Andrews in Fife. Whilst that connection has not been proved conclusively, it is interesting to record a few details of Dr. Bell's contribution to education in the nineteenth century.

Andrew Bell was born in St. Andrews on 27th March 1753. His father was a Bailie, and a barber to trade, who also had a semi-professional interest in various inventions, including a new system of casting type for the printing industry. His mother was of Dutch extraction and somewhat eccentric. As a result of a bursary made available to him from his great-uncle he was able to attend St. Andrews University in 1769. On completion of his education he went to America in 1774, where he acted as tutor to the sons of Carter Braxton, but in 1781 he returned with his students, first to London and then to St. Andrews. After studying for the ministry he went to Madras in India in February 1787 where he held various remunerative posts as Army Chaplain. Two years later he was appointed principal of the Madras Male Orphan Asylum set up by the East India Company. It was here that he first embarked on the monitorial system of education which was later to bring him great acclaim, and financial reward. In retrospect, it is difficult to say whether the Madras system was a genuine experiment in the theory and practice of learning or whether it was forced upon him by the acute shortage of trained teachers. The whole basis of the system was that each pupil should do the maximum for himself, learning at each stage of the proceedings. This idea included not only the more mundane tasks of pupils ruling their own paper and making their own pens, but extended to maintaining collective discipline. More controversially, the teacher instructed the abler pupils personally, leaving it to them to impart the same knowledge to the other pupils, in a vast pupil-teacher hierarchy. In 1796 Bell returned to the United Kingdom and published a report in 1797 under the lengthy title, *An Experiment in Education made at the Male Asylum of Madras; suggesting a System by which a School or Family may teach itself, under the Superintendence of the Master or Parent.* The system was first adopted by St. Botulf's in London in 1799 and spread rapidly to over 12,000 schools in the United Kingdom.

In 1800 Andrew Bell married Agnes Barclay. By then he was forty-seven years of age and, by all accounts, a difficult man to live with. Either through spite or provocation, his wife continued her inventive condemnation of him, long after they were legally separated in 1806. That he was at least cautious with his money is evident from one of her most vehement outbursts: 'To the ape of apes, and the knave of knaves, who is recorded to have once paid a debt, but a small one you may be sure it was that he selected for this wonderful experiment — in fact it was 4½d. Had it been on the other side of 6d. he must have died before he could have achieved so dreadful a sacrifice'.

Towards the end of his life Bell had amassed a huge

fortune, settling a total of £120,000 to found schools on the Madras system in St. Andrews, Edinburgh, Glasgow, Leith, Aberdeen, Inverness, and the Royal Naval School in London. He died on 27th January 1832 and was buried in Westminster Abbey. Although his fortune established several educational institutions, notably the Madras College in St. Andrews, the monitorial system, first introduced by Bell, has long since been discredited. Indeed some would say that it was discredited during Bell's own lifetime.

TRADES MAIDEN HOSPITAL

KIRKWOOD'S MAP OF 1817 provides considerable detail of the various feus of ground extending northwards from Sciennes Loaning (now Sciennes Road). Immediately to the east of Sylvan Place is the site now occupied by the Royal Edinburgh Hospital for Sick Children opened in 1895. In 1817 the property, then known as Rillbank, belonged to William Wilson, whose large L-shaped house sat amidst extensive ornamental gardens and shrubberies. An entrance gate and short driveway came in from Sciennes Loaning, and a much longer and narrower driveway lay to the north. This property was greatly altered in 1855 when it was purchased by the governors of the Trades Maiden Hospital, which had outgrown its previous accommodation at Argyle Square. The Trades Maiden Hospital owes its existence, in part at any rate, to the rivalry which existed between the trades and the merchants of Edinburgh at the beginning of the eighteenth century. The earlier foundation of the Merchant Maiden Hospital, with financial assistance from Mary Erskine, stirred the Incorporated Trades into action, with the result that they purchased premises in Horse Wynd and opened their own hospital in 1704. After incorporation, Mary Erskine also donated a large sum to the continuation of the Trades Maiden Hospital, thus becoming co-founder of two schools with very similar titles. The school remained at Argyle Square from 1739 to 1855 before facing the upheaval of a move to

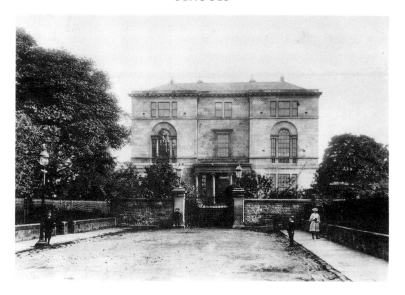

Rillbank, in Rillbank Terrace, occupied by the Trades Maiden Hospital from 1855 to 1892 after which the site was sold for the construction of the new Royal Edinburgh Hospital for Sick Children. Courtesy of Miss Eleanor Hamilton.

the south side of the Meadows. On the opening of the Rillbank premises the Treasurer, John Clark, reported to the governors on 10th September 1855:

> The former residence was not left without a pang of regret on the part of a number of its inmates both old and young. It cannot be doubted, however, that Rillbank is a most eligible site . . . The governors have greatly improved the external appearance so that now it presents to the eye a very chaste and graceful architectural structure. The internal arrangements are also judicious and convenient. The lobby and staircase are peculiarly handsome, the schoolrooms are capacious and well proportioned in their dimensions, the dormatories [sic] are spacious lightsome and well ventilated . . . The institution will possess singular advantages for carrying forward its chief and ultimate

design, namely, to train and educate the daughters and grand-daughters of our decayed fellow craftsmen in the paths of learning and virtue, fitting them for the right discharge of their duties in after life, and, by the blessing of God, for a happy immortality.

The history of the school was reviewed at length in an article by the Rev. Edwin S. Towill in the *Book of the Old Edinburgh Club*, Volume XXVIII. In the section dealing with Rillbank House the author relates details of the daily life and routine of the school. Much of the governors' time appears to have been taken up with drafting regulations or dealing with specific cases of indiscipline. The staff did, however, take a great interest in the well-being of the girls, and modern improvements were brought in as money became available. From a budget which, in the 1880s, must have been stretched beyond endurance, the governors authorised the purchase of gas cookers, sewing machines, croquet sets and elastic chest expanders!

On a broader front the governors were also mindful of their responsibility to respond to changing social conditions and competition from other schools. The syllabus was reorganised with greater emphasis placed on academic achievement, and consideration was given to opening the school for day pupils. This latter suggestion was debated on numerous occasions but eventually rejected. However, in 1876 H.M. Inspector recommended that a headmaster be appointed, resulting in the appointment of Robert Henderson at a salary of £250 per annum.

The school continued at Rillbank until 1892 when the site was sold to the Hospital Authorities for £17,500 in anticipation of a new Royal Hospital for Sick Children. The Trades Maiden Hospital purchased Ashfield, the former house of Henry Younger in Grange Loan for £7,000 and continued its work there. At the present day the Trades Maiden Hospital operates from No. 61 Melville Street, Edinburgh, carrying out the modern equivalent of an idea which originated almost three centuries ago.

The Governor's Meeting Room at Ashfield, home of the Trades Maiden Hospital, in 1968. The photograph shows the Blue Blanket on the far wall, to the right of which is the walnut cabinet made from a tree which grew at Rillbank, and the Offertory Box at the window. Courtesy of Tom Scott of Edinburgh and the Royal Commission on the Ancient and Historical Monuments of Scotland.

ESDAILE

THE LARGE FEU OF GROUND to the east of Kilgraston Road, extending from Dick Place to Grange Loan, has been occupied by the Training Centre of the Royal Bank of Scotland since 1969. The history of the imposing baronial edifice, however, precedes the arrival of the Royal Bank by more than a century.

On 29th November 1810 the Rev. James Esdaile of Montrose was appointed to the East Church at Perth, where he remained as minister until 24th April 1844. During his long ministry he wrote several important works of theology, including *The Evidences of Christian Theology* in 1823 and *Lectures on the Shorter Catechism* in 1829. At the end of his ministry he retired to the Manse at Rescobie near Forfar, the house of his son, the Rev. David Esdaile, where he died in January 1854. His marriage to Margaret Blair of Borgue in 1805 had produced four sons, two of whom, James and David, were instrumental in founding one of Edinburgh's most interesting schools.

James Esdaile, born in 1808, at Montrose, graduated in medicine at Edinburgh University in 1829. He went to India in 1831 to take up a medical appointment with the East India Company, where he became interested in hypnotism, known then as mesmerism, after the German physician Franz Mesmer (1734~1815). Unknown to Esdaile, the subject had also been studied by a Scottish doctor, James Braid, who 'discovered that a genuine self-induced sleep could be brought about by a fixed stare at a bright inanimate object'. Braid's findings, that mesmeric influence was entirely subjective, were published in an important treatise entitled *Neurypnology, or the Rationale of Nervous Sleep* in 1843. Two years prior to the introduction of chloroform by James Young Simpson in 1847, James Esdaile began to use hypnotism to induce anaesthesia for major operations. His first experiment was on 4th April 1845, when he had not actually seen anyone mesmerised before. The patient was a middle-aged Hindu convict, who required two extremely painful surgical operations. When the first operation had been completed without anaesthetic, Esdaile decided to try the mesmeric technique to calm the patient and to alleviate the distress caused by pain and shock. Independent witnesses confirmed that there was 'a complete suspension of sensibility to external impressions of the most painful kind'. Encouraged by the results, Esdaile used the same technique a week later to induce unconsciousness for the second operation. So successful were these methods that he recorded two hundred and sixty-one painless operations, using mesmerism, in the Mesmeric Hospital, Calcutta. In a major operation for amputation, or the removal of a tumour, complete unconsciousness was sometimes achieved in half an hour, whereas other cases took as long as twelve days, complete unconscious-

Esdaile, the Ministers' Daughters' College, in Kilgraston Road was established in 1863 and closed in 1967. The building designed by David Rhind was extended on numerous occasions before becoming the Training Centre of the Royal Bank of Scotland in 1969.

ness only being reached in gradual stages. Between 1845 and 1852 Esdaile produced an impressive list of publications, including *Mesmerism in India and its practical application in surgery and medicine*, in 1846, and *The Introduction of Mesmerism as an anaesthetic and curative agent into the hospitals of India*, in 1852. After twenty years' work dedicated to pioneering new methods of anaesthesia, Esdaile left Calcutta on 1st June 1851 with the comment 'I detested the climate, the country and all its ways from the moment I first set foot in it'. This belated, and surprising, verdict may well have originated in personal tragedy: his young wife of only a few months died on the voyage out in 1831, and his second wife also died in India. His third marriage, in 1851, was spent in Scotland and in Sydenham, near Oxford.

In his latter years, when ill health curtailed physical activity, James discussed with his brother, the Rev. David Esdaile of Rescobie, the idea of founding a school for the daughters of ministers of the Church of Scotland. On 16th October 1858 a brief paragraph appeared in *The Scotsman* under the heading 'Educational Establishment for Clergymen's Daughters', stating that a circular had been sent by the Rev. David Esdaile to the Ministers of the Church of Scotland and the Professors in the Universities of Scotland. The circular advocated a scheme for the education of their daughters 'to give the best, useful, and ornamental education at the smallest possible cost'. It was accompanied by a letter from Dr James Esdaile outlining the scheme and offering his help, but unfortunately he died on 10th January 1859 at the age of fifty before his plan came to fruition.

Implementation of the scheme went ahead with the assistance of several committees. During the General Assembly of 1859 a meeting of interested persons was held and a constitution was approved on 3rd April 1860. An Association was formed for establishing a college with the object that the girls 'should be religiously trained and so familiarised with the details of domestic economy as well as the best production of literature that they shall occupy with honour and advantage whatever position in society may be assigned to them'. Lord Chancellor Campbell was elected President and the Rev. David Esdaile was appointed Secretary of the Council which was to manage the college. On 1st March 1861 the *Home and Foreign Missionary Record of the Church of Scotland* carried the following report:

> The Scheme originates in the wish to mitigate a widespread evil. Owing to their remoteness from good schools, their limited incomes, and the greatly increased cost of female education, the rural clergy, especially, have the greatest difficulty in getting their daughters educated, − their finances not permitting them to employ an accomplished governess . . .

When subscriptions exceeded £4,000 the site in Kilgraston Road was acquired and David Rhind, the architect, was engaged to draw plans for a school to be called the Ministers'

Daughters' College. By 1st October 1863 the College was fully subscribed at fees of £30 per annum, plus two guineas for laundry services. The Council 'selected well-known gentlemen to give instruction in English Literature, French, German, music, writing and arithmetic . . . Professor Bennett was appointed physician and Mr Ayton appointed as dentist'. The Rev. David Esdaile made a plea for continued support: 'knowing the modern tone of feeling in regard to giving freer scope to the powers of the female mind, we think the circumstances of the time favourable to its success'. The school opened on 10th October 1863 with Miss Maclaren as the first Lady Principal, assisted by a small staff for the forty-two pupils who had enrolled.

Rhind's original plan was a regular three-storey, pitched roof structure with the central bay slightly advanced, and flanked on either side by three symmetrical bays. This accommodation was soon found to be inadequate, resulting in a fairly continuous programme of expansion up to the Second World War. As early as 1865 an additional dormitory for ten boarders, a class room, a sick room and a convalescent room were built to the north of the original building. This was followed in 1879 by the dining hall and another dormitory, more than half the cost being borne by J. L. Livingstone, who also financed the construction of the porch, porter's lodge and turret room in 1886. A gymnasium was added in 1893, and two additional storeys were built above the dining hall in 1902, in a slightly different style of architecture. The villas Norwood and Kilroque, to the north of the school, were acquired in 1913 and 1938 respectively. Both these properties gave additional space for boarders and classroom accommodation.

Although the school was opened for the daughters of ministers and university professors, this stipulation was altered in 1871 to include daughters of professional laymen, where all vacancies had not been taken up. No differentiation was made in the education and facilities offered, but the fees for the daughters of ministers and professors continued to be subsidised. In 1926 the school was renamed Esdaile in commemoration of the original founders, and in 1932 the Council was replaced by a Board of Governors. By a fortunate coincidence, however, the initials M.D.C., which had for so long been identified with Ministers' Daughters' College, continued in the school motto MORES DIRIGAT CARITAS (Let Love Direct Your Ways). The school took girls from age eleven to eighteen, giving them a balanced education up to University entrance standard. There was also great emphasis on the social graces and Christian values, supported by a close link with the Church of Scotland, and particularly Grange Church (now Marchmont St. Giles) at the top of Kilgraston Road. Sporting links with other schools were also encouraged, taking full advantage of the extensive playing fields acquired in 1906 in South Oswald Road. One of the highlights was an occasional hockey fixture against the boys of Loretto.

At the outbreak of the Second World War the whole school was evacuated, firstly to Ancrum House in Roxburghshire, and then to Ayton Castle in Berwickshire. During the war years the school building in Kilgraston Road was requisitioned by the War Office. In 1946 Esdaile returned to Edinburgh, bringing with it the memory of the Border hills of Eildon, Minto, Cheviot and Ruberslaw, which became the names of the school houses. Many memories survive from the potentially unsettling times of the war years. Active former pupils now look back, through the pages of Esdaile's *Old Girls' Chronicle*, to the days when crocodiles roamed the streets of Edinburgh. Each walk, with only marginal detours for dire necessity, was referred to by an identity number rather than by a description of the topography. The line, or crocodile, of girls frequently stretched several hundred yards 'policed' at intervals by prefects and members of staff at the rear. For boarders, the standard day began at 7 a.m. to the sound of a hand bell rung by one of the maids. Breakfast was at 7.30 a.m. followed by an inspection of each pupil in front of the prefects. Before the start of classes at 9 a.m. the dormitories had to be tidied and other orderly duties undertaken on a rota basis. Each day there were morning and evening prayers lasting approximately ten minutes in the communal hall on the ground floor. Saturday was a more relaxed day, usually spent on the playing fields, at school outings or on occasional social visits. Sunday was different. The entire school attended the morning service at Grange Church where the front central pews were reserved for Esdaile, with the exception of those girls who aspired to be members of the church choir. Discipline was strict, yet not oppressive. As the greater number of pupils were boarders, the school had the additional responsibility of acting *in loco parentis*. Absences from the school building were granted only after a written request, addressed to the headmistress, was left on a tray outside her study. In retrospect, the temptation to secure a pass by inventing yet another tall story seems to have been based on the naive assumption that the headmistress could not possibly have known that the Dominion Cinema existed. Although at first sight the daily routine may appear to have been unduly strict, in fact it was no different to that of many other boarding schools, where the safety and wellbeing of the pupils is paramount.

The immediate post-war period was dominated by the problems of rising costs, the need to modernise, and the restoration of the interior of the school after fairly rough treatment from 1939 to 1945. Two new classrooms were built adjoining the west side of the gymnasium, helped by a gift of £1,500 from Mrs. Hill Stewart as a Memorial to her father, Professor Milligan of Aberdeen, and her two brothers. Esdaile's headmistress during the war years was Mrs. D. Calembert (1935~1953), and she was followed by Miss B. Forsyth. When Miss Forsyth retired in 1962 the Governors appointed Miss H. M. Ewan from the African Girls' High School in Kikuya, Kenya, an honours graduate of Edinburgh University who also had experience of teaching in other Scottish schools. In 1963 Esdaile celebrated its centenary. Over the years the complement of pupils had grown to 140, of whom 110 were boarders from all parts of Scotland and abroad. The happy traditions and high academic standards of the earlier days were still maintained but in a less formal atmosphere and with a wider variety of activities.

The centenary was marked by two main events. The school celebration was on 27th June 1963 when the Duchess of Gloucester, Patroness of the school, visited Esdaile. In the afternoon the gymnasium was packed with pupils, parents and guests, and a large number of Old Girls were present in the dining-room where they heard a relay of the proceedings. Three dramatic sketches, written by members of staff, were presented illustrating different stages in the school's history. The centenary event organised by the Old Girls' Union was a special dinner in the Caledonian Hotel in October, the month in which the school had opened a century earlier. At the time of the centenary celebrations everything looked set for another hundred years, but in 1967 the Governors announced their intention to close the school for financial reasons. The playing fields in South Oswald Road were sold for housing development and the Kilgraston Road building was bought by the Royal Bank of Scotland. Pupils and staff found places in various schools, mostly in and around Edinburgh.

Despite closure of the school two important bodies survive. Esdaile Old Girls' Union, officially founded in 1900, continues with a membership of five hundred, many of whom have followed the practice of earlier members in making individual and collective gifts to the school. Each year a reunion is held and an issue of the *Old Girls' Chronicle* is produced. The Esdaile Trust, set up from the school funds and sale proceeds of the school building, provides financial assistance for the education of daughters of the manse.

After the closure of Esdaile, the building was acquired by the Royal Bank of Scotland in 1969, as a residential Training Centre for staff from all parts of the United Kingdom. The idea was to centralise training activities, which had previously been located at St. Andrew Square, West Coates, Portobello and Ramsay Lodge. Fortunately, the bank's architect, Mr Pye, was instructed to retain all the external features of the original building, as well as the best parts of the interior. All main services were replaced, a lift was installed, and a small addition made to the east wing for a new fire escape. Three stained glass windows, by a former pupil Marjorie Kemp, have been retained, one in the hall and two on the original staircase. The window in the hall *Saint Columba* is a memorial from the Old Girls' Union to Miss A. P. Robertson, Lady Principal of Esdaile from 1898 to 1918. Of the two staircase windows, the lower one *St. Michael, St. Catherine and Jeanne* includes the school motto MORES DIRIGAT CARITAS, and the higher one, slightly plainer, depicts *Florence Nightingale*.

Additional accommodation is located outside the main building. The school annexe, to the north, has been converted to form a large lecture theatre, a games room, a computer terminal training room, and the cashiers' room, where a model bank branch gives trainees 'live' experience of a teller's duties.

From various vantage points in the extensive grounds it is possible to trace the development of the entire building. The original Rhind elevation (already referred to) is not dated but the first dormitory extension of 1865 has the date on an ornamental water head on the east gable. The turret and porch were added in 1886 using a good match of stone. Finally the date 1902 is carved at the base of a chimney breast on the additional storeys built above the east dining room. Among the many mature trees and shrubs is one of more recent date at the west end of the south terrace, beside which is a commemorative plaque with the following inscription:

THIS ACER TREE WAS PRESENTED TO THE COLLEGE
BY THE ESDAILE OLD GIRLS' UNION TO MARK THE
OCCASION OF THEIR VISIT ON 26 MAY 1973

F

CRAIGMOUNT

THE IMPOSING PILLARS at the entrance to the modern housing development at Wyvern Park in Dick Place once gave access to Craigmount, a distinctive group of buildings constructed around 1864. Originally the gate pillars were set much closer together in alignment with the south pavement of Dick Place, but they were repositioned to accommodate increased traffic when the houses of Wyvern Park were built. The old carriage driveway swept round a circular pond to the front of White House, a massive structure of three main storeys with turrets, dominated by a high square tower on the south-east corner. Directly south of White House was the more elaborate Red House, with its imposing flight of stairs, chevron string courses, chimneys like sentries, and south-facing balconies at second-floor level. The architect was F. T. Pilkington whose individual style is easily recognised from some of his surviving works, notably Egremont or Grange Park House in Dick Place, and Barclay Church at Bruntsfield Links. Detailed plans and drawings of Pilkington's work were exhibited by the Royal Incorporation of Architects in Scotland during the 1989 Edinburgh International Festival. Among the major works exhibited were: the Royal Scottish National Hospital, Larbert, 1861; Trinity Church, Irvine, 1861–1863; Barclay Church, 1862; Egremont House 1865–70; and perhaps the most grandiose of all, Craigend Park, Liberton, 1867–1869. Also included were examples of Pilkington's lesser-known domestic architecture, notably Parkend Flats, Penicuik, 1860, and a tenement building in Edinburgh on the corner of Fountainbridge and Grove Street, in 1864.

Craigmount, in Dick Place, was first used as a boarding school for boys, established by James Sime around 1865. He also ran a day school from 1881 to 1889 for about forty boys at South Park on the corner of Blackford Avenue and Grange Terrace. South Park remained in the Sime family until 1895 after which it was occupied by numerous persons until the

Craigmount School in Dick Place showing Red House on the left (designed by F. T. Pilkington) and White House on the right. Craigmount was a boys' school from 1865 to 1900 after which it became a girls' school until evacuation to Scone Palace in 1939. Courtesy of Miss E. R. Landells.

end of the century. It was bought in 1901 by John Ewart, Writer to the Signet, who sold the building to the British Geological Survey in 1928. In 1891 James Sime was joined at Craigmount by Peirce De Lacy Johnstone, M.A. Oxon, M.R.A.S., Barrister-at-Law who advertised extensively as a teacher of Oriental Languages and Indian Law, preparing students for the Indian Civil Service in Persian, Arabic, Sanskrit and Hindustani. Johnstone was a Boden Sanskrit Scholar at Oxford and a High Proficiency Prizeman in Calcutta for Persian and Sanskrit. Sime and Johnstone continued at Craigmount until 1900 when it became a girls' school.

A detailed account of Craigmount Girls' School is available thanks to research undertaken by an ex-pupil and member of staff, Miss Mary Fraser, whose work was published in the January 1987 edition of the *Scots Magazine*. The origins of the school go back to 1884 when the five Misses Gossip opened their first school in Blantyre Terrace.

After occupying the Lodge in Forbes Road and Falcon Hall, off Morningside Road, they moved to Craigmount in 1900. In the late 1920s and the 1930s the two main buildings, Red House and White House, contained the dormitories and classrooms of various sizes. There was a swimming pool in the White House which was floored over in the winter to create classroom 6. The annexe housed the gymnasium *cum* assembly room. Each dormitory contained about six beds, hung with curtains, but girls were expected to share storage accommodation with at least one other boarder. Classes varied greatly in size, usually between ten and fifteen pupils each, with about fifteen full-time staff, including the Principal. In addition to the full-time staff there were visiting teachers for elocution, art and music. Non-teaching staff included a matron, assistant matron, cook, maids, gardener, and also a secretary. The academic curriculum followed that provided by most other secondary schools, in addition to which there was dancing and numerous sporting activities. These included hockey, netball, tennis and cricket, the last played at the Carlton Cricket Club in Grange Loan (reached through a small doorway from Craigmount's kitchen garden). A few girls also went horse riding on the Braid Hills under instruction from Liberton Stables and later from Moncur's Establishment at Belford Bridge. Extra-curricular activities included concerts, visits to the theatre and exhibitions, and, for the senior girls, an annual school trip to the Continent. Sport was not permitted on Sundays, the highlight of the day being a walk to one of the local churches for the morning service. Sunday afternoons were spent reading, writing letters, or walking 'in crocodile' to the Blackford Hill or Braid Hills. In the evening the more senior girls returned to church.

The total roll at the school increased gradually to one hundred and fifty pupils, ranging in age from less than five to eighteen years. Latterly there were more day pupils than boarders, divided into three houses, Oakwood, Homehill and Lauderfield. School uniform consisted of a dark coloured

Margaret Kinmont Ross, Principal of Craigmount School in Dick Place, born 1883 died 1954, photographed on her graduation day in Edinburgh in April 1905. Courtesy of Alastair K. Ross.

gym costume, white square-necked, long-sleeved blouse, black stockings, blazer or navy blue coat, a hat with the school badge, and gloves. In the 1930s the colour of the school uniform was changed to green.

The school remained under the control of the Misses Gossip until their retirement in 1911 when they were succeeded by Miss Macdonald and Mrs Henderson. In 1921 Miss Adamson and her sister, who were previously heads of St. Elizabeth's School in Rothesay Terrace, took over Craigmount. After the death of one of the sisters, the other remained at the school with Mrs Landells as headmistress. The oak-leaf badge, and the motto, EX ANIMO SICUT DOMINO (FROM THE HEART, AS TO THE LORD), were introduced from St. Elizabeth's to replace the earlier motto FERIO TEGO (I STRIKE, I DEFEND), which originated in Mr Sime's boys' school. In 1932 Miss Margaret Kinmont Ross became headmistress, described by Miss Mary Fraser in her article as 'a woman of wide culture, sincerely religious, and with a great affection for and understanding of young people — about whom, however, she had no illusions'. Under her guidance the school was evacuated to Scone Palace in 1939 where it remained until 1952. It then transferred to Minto House, near Hawick, but unfortunately closed in 1966 for economic reasons. A reunion of former pupils and staff was held at the Post House Hotel in Edinburgh in November 1985, and again at Scone Palace in October 1988.

Perhaps more than any other member of staff of her time Margaret Kinmont Ross epitomises the story of Craigmount. She is referred to in Daphne Rae's autobiography *A World Apart* as 'an eccentric and delightful person', from whom Daphne received great support and encouragement during her own traumatic childhood. Miss Ross retired from Craigmount in 1949 to a house in Grange Loan Gardens almost within reach of the old school grounds in Dick Place. In 1954 she died in a motor accident on Shap in Cumbria at the age of seventy-one.

EDINBURGH SOUTHERN INSTITUTION: STRATHEARN COLLEGE

RICHARD DALZIEL GRAHAM began his long and distinguished career in education in fairly humble surroundings. In 1866, as a thirty-year-old teacher of English, he was resident at No. 6 Marmion Terrace (now part of Morningside Road near its junction with Church Hill). It seems possible that he may have taken some classes at Baillie's School, which was established for many years at No. 4 Marmion Terrace. In 1870 Mr Graham removed to No. 18 Lonsdale Terrace where he continued to build up his reputation as a competent teacher and administrator. His first big opportunity came in 1878 when he opened his own school, the Edinburgh Southern Institution for the Board and Education of Young Ladies at No. 11 Strathearn Road. Copies of the prospectus were made freely available giving details of various courses with fees ranging from twelve to twenty-eight guineas per session, and sixty guineas per session for board. His introductory comments revealed that he had been one of the early masters at the Ministers' Daughters' College shortly after it opened in 1863:

EDINBURGH SOUTHERN INSTITUTION

FOR

BOARD AND EDUCATION OF YOUNG LADIES

11 STRATHEARN ROAD

PRINCIPAL – R. D. GRAHAM

TO BE OPENED ON THE 1ST OCTOBER 1878

THIS INSTITUTION is intended to meet the requirements of the large and growing population in the Southern Suburbs of Edinburgh, and will be under the entire management of Mr Richard Dalziel Graham, who for the last thirteen years has been Master of the English Language and Literature in the Ministers Daughters College and many of the principal Ladies Boarding Schools of this City.

Mr Graham will be assisted by teachers of the highest standing in their several departments, and by an efficient staff of residents and other governesses.

In 1881 Mr Graham extended his school into the adjacent property, No. 12 Strathearn Place, and in 1885 he acquired No. 10 which had previously been occupied by the Hon. Charles Baillie and then John Horsburgh, the photographer and portrait painter. Baillie's house was originally a square two-storey building with a central ornamented doorway but Graham arranged for an additional storey to be built. Extensive internal alterations were made to form toilets and classrooms, several of which were intended as music rooms. Further expansion took place in 1890 when the college occupied Nos. 10, 11 and 12, and altered its name to Strathearn College. In the following year Mr Graham was elected a Fellow of the Royal Society of Edinburgh, but he does not appear to have retired until around 1907 shortly after his seventieth birthday. He remained at No. 11 but No. 10 was acquired by Miss E. C. G. Mitchell who re-advertised Strathearn College as 'a practical training school for cookery and domestic economy for resident and visiting pupils under the Principal Miss Mitchell, first class Diploma, formerly at 1A Kilgraston Road'. After the death of Mr Graham on 12th September 1920 Miss Mitchell took over Nos. 10, 11 and 12, improved internal communication between the buildings and reconstructed the demonstration room to the rear. She appears to have been a lady of considerable business acumen, having acquired two other properties which she used as boarding accommodation. The first, in 1926, was Ardvahn at No. 10 Palmerston Road which had previously been used by St. Trinnean's School before it removed to St. Leonard's House. The other was Varrich House at No. 7 Church Hill, now occupied by the Church of Scotland as an eventide home.

Strathearn College continued up to the beginning of the Second World War, but in 1941 the buildings were taken over by the Army. Since then it has been used as a Medical Reception Station for the Edinburgh area caring for non-acute sick personnel.

St. Trinnean's

ON 4TH OCTOBER 1922 sixty girls met in a large room at No. 10 Palmerston Road with little or no idea of what it was like to be the first pupils in a school whose name became almost a household word. St. Trinnean's was established by Miss C. Fraser Lee, a single-minded educationalist, with a determination to succeed with the Dalton system of learning. This

Film still of Alastair Sim as the headmistress in *The Belles of St. Trinians* produced by Frank Launder and Sidney Gilliat.

revolutionary system of education attracted a great deal of attention and criticism, to the point where it was said that St. Trinnean's was 'the school where they do what they like'. In fact, discipline was probably stricter than was first imagined, the emphasis being on self-discipline rather than the enforced variety.

The school was divided into four Senior Houses, Whithorn, Monenn, Clagrinnie and Kilninian, whose duty it was to elect two girls each, as representatives for the Senate, presided over by the Head Girl. The Senate drew up Rules of Convenience and Danger Rules and took an active part in the maintenance of self-discipline. The Dalton system allowed an element of choice in arranging study time throughout the day. After roll call at 9 a.m. the girls went to the various Study Rooms of their choice and were free to move from one subject to another during the course of the morning. In order to maintain control each pupil was provided with sufficient work for a month, arranged into weeks, with a calendar on which she marked the time given to each subject. Each week's assignment was checked by the House Mistress to ensure that an adequate time had been allotted to each subject. If there was time left over, this was taken up by the system of Opportunity Work, preferably devoted to the girl's weakest subject. In this way Miss Lee maintained that she developed the pupils' sense of responsibility and prepared them more adequately for the freedom which they would find in the colleges and universities.

St. Trinnean's remained at Palmerston Road until 1925, when it moved to St. Leonard's House, near Dalkeith Road, designed by John Lessels for Thomas Nelson, the Edinburgh printer. At the beginning of the Second World War St. Trinnean's was evacuated to Gala House in Galashiels, but owing to lack of accommodation and the retirement of Miss Lee, the school closed in September 1946.

Had the story ended there, St. Trinnean's would probably have been like many other small private schools of its day, remembered only by a dwindling number of ex-teachers and former pupils. That was not, however, the fate of St. Trinnean's. In 1941 a curious coincidence led to the school's name being used with the slightly different spelling of St. Trinians. The Johnston family, whose two daughters attended St. Trinnean's in Edinburgh, had been evacuated to Kirkcudbright where they met Sapper Searle serving with H.M. Forces. By way of a domestic joke, Searle demonstrated his considerable artistic ability by drawing a cartoon giving his idea of the school attended by the Johnston daughters. Although the cartoon was published by *Lilliput*, nothing more was heard of Searle's work until 1946, when he was eventually released from a Japanese prisoner-of-war camp. When he returned to Britain at the end of the War, *Lilliput* produced his cartoons and brought St. Trinians to the attention of the world. The story was given an even greater impetus in 1954 when the renowned Edinburgh actor Alastair Sim played the part of the headmistress in the film *The Belles of St. Trinians* produced by Frank Launder and Sidney Gilliat.

Whilst no one would doubt the artistic and humorous talents of Alastair Sim and Ronald Searle, the St. Trinians story must have received a fairly mixed reception in Edinburgh, in the 1950s. To set the record straight Miss C. Fraser Lee wrote *The Real St. Trinnean's* in 1962 giving an account of the history of the school from 1922 to 1946. Of Ronald Searle she says, 'I hope we may [meet] one day, for I am glad he has been so successful, but often wish he had chosen a more ordinary name like St. Mary's or St. Catherine's, but then the strange Gaelic name of St. Trinnean may have appealed to him, and no one believed that a school with such a name existed'.

The original school building at No. 10 Palmerston Road has been in private occupation for many years.

THE GRANGE HOME SCHOOL

ACCORDING TO *THE BUILDINGS OF SCOTLAND – EDINBURGH* the house known as Dunard at No. 123 Grange Loan was designed by Robert R. Raeburn around 1865. Whilst there is no reason to dispute the date of Raeburn's drawings, it was not until around 1875 that the house appeared on any map.

The first recorded occupant, in 1876, was John Sime, an Edinburgh stockbroker, who sold the property around 1886 to Lt. Col. A. Borthwick, Late Rifle Brigade, Chief Constable of Midlothian and West Lothian. No doubt civic receptions at Dunard were continued on an even grander scale from 1895 when the house was bought by Sir Robert Cranston, Lord Provost of Edinburgh, renowned for his lavish entertainment of foreign visitors to the City. Sir Robert entered the Town Council in 1892, was City Treasurer from 1899 to 1902, and held the position of Lord Provost from 1903 to 1906. One of his great interests was the Volunteer Movement where he started as a lieutenant in the Queen's Edinburgh Rifles and rose to be Brigadier-General of the 1st Lothians Brigade. He was knighted by King Edward VII in May 1903 and made a K.C.V.O. at the Volunteer Review of 1905. In 1923 he obtained the Freedom of the City but died a few months later at the age of eighty. Sir Robert did not live at Dunard in his later life, but sold the property in 1913 to David Mitchell, who in turn sold it to James S. Aikman in 1920.

Also in 1920, Mrs Edith Morley Smith bought No. 9 Strathearn Place for herself and her four young children, having been recently widowed following the First World War. She opened Grange Home School in the premises and spent many years building up a successful boarding and day school for young children, whose parents were either abroad or were living in remote parts of the country where suitable education was not readily at hand. As the size and influence of the school increased, Mrs Morley Smith was anxious to secure more commodious accommodation in the Grange district. When Mr Aikman put Dunard on the market in 1933 Mrs Morley Smith purchased it and transferred the school to the new premises. For the next few years the school was conducted along similar lines to that at Strathearn Place. However, that stability was temporarily affected, along with most other schools, in 1939, when the staff and pupils were evacuated, first to Berwickshire and then to Comrie. Dunard

A 'family' group round the piano led by Miss Joan Morley Smith, Principal of Grange Home School, c. 1965 (Courtesy of Mrs A. Wilkinson (née Morley Smith).

was requisitioned by the War Department. At the end of the War, Mrs Morley Smith returned to Dunard only to find that the building had been badly damaged by wartime occupation. Following a breakdown in her health, she retired in 1946, leaving the running of the school in the hands of her daughter, Miss Joan Morley Smith.

During the next three decades Grange Home School increased its roll to almost one hundred and fifty pupils, between the ages of three and eleven years. Although day pupils were taken from age three, boarders were not normally accepted until age four. Girls remained at the school until age eleven when most of them went on to George Watson's Ladies' College, St. Hilary's, St. Denis's or Esdaile: boys moved on at age seven to such schools as Loretto and

Cargilfield. There were a nursery class, two kindergarten classes and three junior classes with a staff of seven full-time teachers. Part-time staff visited the school to teach dancing, games, art and music. The non-teaching staff consisted of a bursar, a matron, assistant matron, cook and domestics to cater for the thirty boarders of various ages. A gardener was also employed to maintain the extensive ground to the south of the school building, frequently used for school sports and other outdoor activities. Every morning all pupils, dressed in the school uniform of fawn and turquoise, congregated on the main staircase in the hallway for morning prayers before starting to their day's work.

When the school closed in 1973 the building was let to St. Margaret's, who used it as their Senior Boarding House. St. Margaret's bought the building in 1976 and later sold it to developers who converted the original house, a listed building, into luxury flats and built four other blocks in the garden ground.

During the Grange Home School's occupation of Dunard, a mahogany bench, which sat in the vestibule for many years, was reputed to have been sat on by Edward VII, without the staff having any idea of the origin of the story. Recent research has identified Lord Provost Cranston as one of the early owners and he was knighted by Edward VII in 1903.

SCIENNES SCHOOL

FOR ALMOST A CENTURY Sciennes School has provided first-class education for many thousands of children from the South Side of the city. The building was designed in 1889 by Robert Wilson, the School Board architect, and opened on 1st March 1892. Day classes for children began almost simultaneously with the lesser-known Sciennes Evening School for Adults.

The first session of the Evening School attracted an attendance of sixty-six for which a total grant of £29: 4/−

was received. Despite this meagre subsidy, attendances rose to over one hundred in the second session, by which time the headmaster, Andrew Tait, had the assistance of five teachers. Evening work was divided into two periods: Arithmetic, Science, Shorthand and French were taught between 8.00 p.m. and 8.45 p.m.; and English and Book-keeping were given a slightly longer period from 8.45 p.m. to 9.35 p.m. The authorities were not long in checking to see that the grant was being properly applied: on 7th February 1894 Councillor Telfer, a Member of the Committee appointed by the Town Council, visited the school 'to enquire and report as to how the Residue Grant voted to the School Board for promoting Technical Instruction in the Evening Schools was being spent'. A satisfactory report followed, within a few months of which two extra teachers were required to deal with an attendance which had by then reached almost two hundred.

At the beginning of the twentieth century the curriculum was greatly strengthened and the work reorganised under the new headmaster, James Hart. An art teacher was employed in addition to four teachers for commercial subjects and four for technical subjects. A strong link was also developing between the Evening School and Principal Laurie of Heriot Watt College. By 1908 the roll was approximately three hundred, and new classes were being introduced, to include printing and machine construction. At the 1909 examinations, sixty-nine pupils qualified for Heriot Watt College in art, business procedure, bookkeeping, building construction, machine construction and arithmetic.

At the outbreak of war in 1914 the Evening School included several subjects associated with the war effort. A military class in map reading and field sketching was introduced for the men of the Royal Scots, who were billeted at James Gillespie's School. This facility was later extended to the Argyll and Sutherland Highlanders, but by the following year an Order was issued by the School Board, dated 24th February 1916, to the effect that all evening classes were to be cancelled in view of the new lighting restrictions. Instead, the classes were held from 3.00 p.m. to 5.00 p.m. on Saturdays, when the effect of the blackout restrictions was less severe. In 1918 evening classes were reintroduced with seventy-three females seeing their way to enlisting for War Time Demonstrations in Cookery and Voluntary Rationing.

Immediately after the First World War the Evening School staff totalled twenty-one, among whom was James McCracken of 22 Jordan Lane, who became an almost legendary character as the swimming master at Sciennes School Baths from 1911 until his retirement in 1949. As subjects were adjusted to peacetime requirements, specific instructions were issued to the school to re-establish communication with demobilised soldiers regarding possible subjects of interest. An impressive curriculum was set for the start of the 1919 Evening School session: a course in salesmanship was offered by John Thomson of Jenners; a police class was headed by Superintendent Calder of Braid Place Police Station; there was a gardening class for allotment holders; and perhaps most ambitious of all were Andrew Macindoe's elocution lessons for shop assistants. A significant number of male pupils were also seen from time to time by Major Meikle of the North British Rubber Works who arranged for apprentices to attend classes. In the late 1920s the Edinburgh rabbi, the Rev. Dr Daiches, father of Professor David Daiches, also held classes in Hebrew and religious subjects, assisted by a small staff.

Although the records for Sciennes Evening School are extant up until 1931, there is no documentary evidence of its existence after that date. Nevertheless, evening classes in various forms have continued to the present day.

The day school for children, between the ages of five and fourteen, opened on 1st March 1892 under the headmaster, Samuel MacCulloch Murray, and his first assistant, Thomas James Robertson, from Leven Public School in Fife. First to be enrolled among five hundred children was the headmaster's own son. Teachers were appointed from several well-known Edinburgh schools, including Dean, Canongate, Castlehill, New Street, Bristo and St. Leonards, but further recruitment was required as enrolment exceeded one thousand pupils. The school was formally opened on 3rd June 1892 by the Right Honourable Lord Reay in the presence of the chairman and various members of the School Board. With enthusiasm probably outstripping ability, the pupils provided a musical programme, followed by an address and an exhibition of swimming under the direction of Sergeant Dodds.

The first session was beset with the usual problems of setting up a large school in a comparatively short time. Parts of the building were unfinished and the unexpectedly high enrolment meant that classes could not be kept to realistic numbers until more teachers were appointed. Tragedy also struck. Four pupils died of scarlet fever and many more were affected with measles and other child ailments. When the headmaster's own children contracted whooping cough he offered to leave his home at No. 70 Thirlestane Road until the outbreak was controlled, but the School Board advised him that it would not be necessary to do so. Despite the difficulties H.M. Inspector's Report dated 5th May 1893 stated that 'this admirably equipped school has made a brilliant start . . .' Over the next decade the staff increased to seventeen teachers (plus seven pupil teachers) in the juvenile department, and nine teachers (plus three pupil teachers) in the infant department. Mr Murray, the first headmaster, retired on 23rd December 1903, his logbook reflecting some of the day-to-day events of the school: 22.3.1900 — serious dispute between the Infant Mistress and other staff members eventually referred to the School Board; 21.12.1900 — school closed today for the holidays and for the century; 23.1.1901 — school closed today as a tribute of reverent respect to the memory of Queen Victoria.

In the first two decades of the twentieth century the daily logs record the impact on the school of national and international events. A short service was held on the afternoon of 19th May 1910 for the King's funeral the following day, but on 23rd June 1911 grief gave way to jubilation for the Coronation of King George V:

> This being Coronation Day the pupils met in the school at 1.30 p.m. by order of the School Board, then marched to the East Meadows and engaged in games and races till interrupted by rain, when they re-assembled in the school and were addressed by the Headmaster. Each child was presented with a bag of cakes and a box of rock. After singing the National Anthem and giving three cheers for the King and Queen the children were dismissed.

A holiday was given on 24th June 1914 in celebration of the 600th anniversary of the Battle of Bannockburn, a sentiment which took on a different meaning at the outbreak of the First World War. Warrender Park School was requisitioned by the War Office, necessitating the transfer of children to Sciennes where a special double-shift system was introduced. Classes, alternating on consecutive weeks, were held from 8.30 a.m. to 12.30 p.m. for Sciennes pupils, and 12.45 p.m. to 4.45 p.m. for Warrender Park children. The infant classes of both schools were taught in the mornings and arrangements were made to provide free dinners for poor children or children whose fathers were on active service. At the end of 1915 the headmaster Mr Crocket resigned through ill health. Although his position was filled almost immediately, the new headmaster, Major Whitton (later Colonel) did not take up his duties until the end of the War.

During the 1920s the number of Jewish pupils attending Sciennes reflected the growing Jewish population on the South Side of Edinburgh. The headmaster made it known to the staff that absences were likely at various dates in the Jewish calendar, an explanation of which has been provided by Professor David Daiches. There are five main festivals in the Jewish year: Passover, Feast of Weeks, the Jewish New

Year, the Day of Atonement and the Feast of Tabernacles. Passover commemorates the exodus of the Jews from Egypt, and Shevuoth or the Feast of Weeks commemorates the giving of the Law to Moses on Mount Sinai. The New Year is a very solemn day preceding by ten days the Day of Atonement (Yom Kippur), the most solemn day in the Jewish calendar on which the Jewish community fasts and asks for forgiveness of sins. Finally there is the Feast of Tabernacles which commemorates the Israelites' sojourn in the wilderness on the way to the Promised Land. It is also the harvest thanksgiving festival. As the Jewish calendar is geared to the lunar month and not the solar calendar, these various festivals appear on different dates in the school logs.

In the months prior to the outbreak of the Second World War detailed plans were made at Sciennes for emergency situations. By the end of March 1939 all pupils had been fitted with gas-masks and letters had been sent to parents giving them details of the intended evacuation scheme. On 2nd September the first evacuation took place: 827 persons were registered and marched to Blackford Hill Station en route for Cupar in Fife. Only 425 of the total number evacuated were schoolchildren, the remaining contingent consisting of: children under school age 188; parents 147; helpers 29; Sciennes School teachers 21; other school teachers 17. Within a few weeks of leaving Edinburgh some confusion was evident as to the true intention of evacuation. More than three hundred pupils had declined evacuation and were being taught in groups of not more than twelve in various private houses. Air-raid warnings were still sounding throughout the district as evacuees began to return to their homes. Air-raid shelters were built firstly in the playground and then in the basement of the school building. Although there was no widespread damage in the vicinity, several logbook entries convey the fervour of the moment: 28.6.40 — air raid on Tuesday night which interfered with the children's sleep and the attendance was poor on Wednesday; 12.7.40 — school holidays with a warning to the teachers that they might be recalled if the Government gives the order for registered children to be evacuated; 11.10.40 — the dropping of bombs on houses in Marchmont Crescent on Monday night affected many of our pupils though none of them were injured; 30.6.41 — staff volunteer for fire-watchers in school at night.

After sharing in the nation's anxiety and tragedy for almost six years, the school joined in the celebrations of Victory in Europe with a holiday on 8th and 9th May 1945. A few days later, on 16th May, all the schoolchildren and the staff turned out to see the Royal motorcade drive down Grange Road on its peripheral tour of the city. At the final cessation of hostilities, the children, unaware of the damage which had already been done, waited anxiously to be reintroduced to their fathers as they returned from the front. Less than a year later each child received a specially printed message from the King urging them 'to feel proud of parents and elder brothers and sisters who by their courage, endurance and enterprise brought victory'. As late as December 1950 the trauma of the war years was still evident in the list of official engagements: the headmaster was invited to the City Chambers to hear an address by the Lord Provost who appealed to the headmasters and headmistresses of Edinburgh to support the Lord Mayor of London's Fund 'to express the country's thanks for the Gift Parcels from the Commonwealth during the Second World War'.

By 1953 the Commonwealth, and the school, were in more buoyant mood for the Coronation of Queen Elizabeth II, celebrated by the pupils of Sciennes at a special service held in Argyle Place Church. Afterwards, mugs and sweets were distributed — followed by three days' holidays.

In 1989 the total number of pupils at Sciennes was 543, between the ages of five and twelve, 163 of them coming from outwith the school's own catchment area of Newington and the Grange. The school's philosophy of working closely with parents and guardians finds expression in the Sciennes Association, an extended parent/teacher association which

Happy smiling faces in the playground of Sciennes School, 1989.
Courtesy of *The Scotsman* Publications Ltd.

encourages membership of everyone interested in the
wellbeing of the school.

Sciennes Primary School will celebrate its centenary in
1992. Whilst few people would suggest that the school has
run for almost a century without some difficulties, it is
interesting to recall the 1892 report which stated that 'this
admirably equipped school has made a brilliant start'. There
is every indication that the school, under the present
headteacher Mrs Maureen Pollock, is admirably placed to
continue that tradition into its next century. The 1988 report
by H.M. Inspector of Schools stated that 'The headteacher
provided very effective leadership and, ably supported by
the depute headteacher and the two assistant headteachers,
she had made considerable progress in devising policies and
guidelines to shape the curriculum'.

CHAPTER 8

HOSPITALS AND VETERINARY COLLEGE

IN THE COMPARATIVELY SMALL GEOGRAPHICAL AREA OF SCIENNES AND THE GRANGE, three hospitals have been established in response to very different aspects of the health and welfare of the community. Perhaps the best known is the Royal Edinburgh Hospital for Sick Children established in 1860 in modest premises in Lauriston Lane, and transferred first to Meadowside House in 1863, and then to the purpose-built red sandstone building in Sciennes Road in 1895. At almost the opposite end of the patient age-scale, the Edinburgh Hospital for Incurables was established in 1874 and given a substantial donation of £10,000 from the Trustees of the late John Alexander Longmore. As a result the new Longmore Hospital, designed by Kinnear and Peddie, was built in Salisbury Place, and opened in 1880. The youngest hospital is St. Raphael's in Blackford Avenue, opened by the British Red Cross in 1919, and staffed by the Sisters of the Little Company of Mary to care for severely disabled servicemen from the First World War. It continued in that capacity for the first decade, after which civilian patients were gradually introduced. St. Raphael's was for long the only Catholic general hospital in the East of Scotland, but in 1982 it was converted into a Nursing Home under the name of St. Raphael's Housing Association.

In addition to the three hospitals in the district, Summerhall was chosen in the early part of the twentieth

The ornate stone plaque commemorating the Lady Caroline Charteris Wing at the Royal Edinburgh Hospital for Sick Children. Photograph by Phyllis M. Cant.

century as the new home of the Royal Dick Veterinary College which had previously been in Clyde Street. William Dick's determination to elevate veterinary medicine to its rightful place among other medical and scientific disciplines is one of Edinburgh's great nineteenth-century success stories.

THE ROYAL EDINBURGH HOSPITAL FOR SICK CHILDREN

THE ROYAL EDINBURGH HOSPITAL FOR SICK CHILDREN in Sciennes Road was opened on 31st October 1895, but it had been in existence at other locations in the city for thirty-five years prior to that date. The story of its founding, and subsequent development into one of the country's foremost hospitals, is related in two recent publications. The comprehensive centenary story, *The Royal Edinburgh Hospital for Sick Children*, by Douglas Guthrie and other contributors, was published in 1960, and in 1970 the *Royal Hospital for Sick Children Edinburgh* was published to mark seventy-five years at Sciennes Road.

In 1860 life in the Old Town of Edinburgh was completely different to the old-world charm portrayed by the now popular prints of old Edinburgh. Behind the romantic imagery of the old stone and timber-faced buildings lay a labyrinth of sub-standard houses, saturated by disease, destitution and despair. Infancy was no protection, with mortality rates seven times higher than they were a century later. Although some restrictions had been introduced to regulate the employment of children, their continued state of ill-health was inextricably linked to the social problems of the day — poverty, lack of nourishment, drunkenness and a complete absence of even basic hygiene. Compelling case studies were included in 'The Origins of Paediatric Surgery in Edinburgh' which F. H. Robarts presented to the Royal College of Surgeons in Edinburgh as the 1968 James J. Mason Brown Memorial Lecture. Mr Robarts referred to Charles Dickens' recollection of an Edinburgh case, when he (Dickens) was delivering an after-dinner speech in 1857 in aid of funds for the Sick Children's Hospital at Great Ormond Street, in London. Dickens recalled that in circumstances of great poverty and squalor he found a sick child lying in an old egg box in an Edinburgh close:

> A little feeble, wan, sick child with his little wasted face, and his little hot warm hands folded over his breast, and his little bright attentive eyes, I can see him now as I have seen him for several years looking steadily at us . . . There he lay quite quiet, quite

patient, saying never a word. He seldom cried, the mother said, he seldom complained; 'he lay there seemin' to wonder what it was a' aboot'.

Against this background it might seem surprising that the idea of founding a hospital to deal exclusively with the health and welfare of children met with such serious opposition. It was pointed out that there were already several hospitals dealing with patients of all ages, and 'that children, after all, were only adults in miniature'! Comparison with other British and European cities placed Edinburgh in an unenviable position, despite its existing reputation as a medical centre. The earliest institution for the treatment of sick children in Britain was the Dispensary in London founded in 1769: L'Hôpital des Enfants Malades was reconstituted in Paris in 1802; and similar hospitals followed in St. Petersburg in 1834, Vienna in 1837 and Budapest in 1839. The first children's hospital in Britain was the Great Ormond Street Hospital for Sick Children founded in London in 1852 by Dr Charles West.

In Edinburgh, the challenge was met by the unique contribution of two doctors, Dr Charles Wilson, a distinguished Kelso physician, later resident in Edinburgh, and Dr John Smith, the pioneer Edinburgh Surgeon-Dentist who was also involved in the founding of the Edinburgh Dental Hospital. Dr Charles Wilson concentrated on persuading the medical profession that something had to be done, and Dr John Smith appealed to the public at large, without whose financial support nothing was possible. It was Wilson's series of articles published in the *Edinburgh Medical Journal* between 1856 and 1859 which acted as a springboard to the lofty heights of the medical profession:

> We must interpret the signs of the period and the need for the establishment of a better system of instruction in diseases of children. In the cause of science and humanity, we cannot afford to fall behind the rest of the world.

Meantime Dr John Smith wrote to *The Scotsman* on 24th February 1859, his classical pseudonym 'Sigma, M.D.' being sufficiently vague to conceal his true identity:

> Why is it that in Edinburgh we have no hospital for the reception of children labouring under disease. Hospitals for the adult sick are not suitable for children and in Edinburgh, of all places, no one seems to have thought of the misery which poverty adds to sickness during infancy. Another ground of appeal lies in the fact that the Edinburgh Medical School possesses no adequate means for teaching practically the important subject of children's diseases.

On 4th March the first of many gifts was received, anonymously, offering £100 which 'Sigma, M.D.' acknowledged in a further letter dated 10th March. In it he also disclosed his identity. The scene was set. On 5th May 1859 a Public Meeting was held in the Freemasons' Hall in George Street under the chairmanship of the Rev. Dr Hodson, Rector of Edinburgh Academy, at which it was decided to set up a hospital in Edinburgh for the relief of sick children, and to act as a centre for the instruction of medical students and nurses in the care of children and the diseases of childhood.

The first priority was to secure suitable premises. Well-intentioned offers of accommodation from the Royal Infirmary and Surgeons' Hall were considered but declined. Incorporation with Chalmers Hospital for the Sick and Hurt was also discussed but came to nothing as the Trustees for the benefactor, George Chalmers, concluded that the terms of the Trust envisaged a hospital for adults and not one solely for children. Eventually a suitable house, subject to a five-year lease at an annual rent of £100, was found at No. 7 Lauriston Lane to the west of the Royal Infirmary. Ironically, agreement was reached only after several objections were overruled — one from the Merchant Maiden Hospital nearby. The first members of staff included the house surgeon Dr

King George VI and Queen Elizabeth during a visit to the Royal Edinburgh Hospital for Sick Children in Sciennes Road, 1946. From *The Royal Edinburgh Hospital for Sick Children* by Douglas Guthrie and others, published by E & S Livingstone Ltd.

William Robertson, and the matron Mrs Booty from Great Ormond Street Children's Hospital in London. Among a handful of other staff were two nurses, each to be paid a sum 'not exceeding £8 a year, including tea money, beer money, and washing money'.

The hospital opened without any special ceremony on 15th February 1860, providing facilities for twelve patients which was doubled within a very short time. No. 7 had never been thought of as a permanent home, however, and within three years the search was resumed for more suitable premises. Fortunately, the directors did not have far to look. Meadowside House, a large four-storey detached building at the foot of Lauriston Lane, was purchased for £2,150 and was opened as the Royal Edinburgh Hospital for Sick Children on 18th May 1863 by Lord Provost Charles Lawson. Royal Patronage was granted by Queen Victoria a few weeks before the opening, an honour which was never bestowed on the Hospital for Sick Children, Great Ormond Street. Much of the purchase price for the Royal Edinburgh Hospital for Sick Children had been raised at a bazaar in the Music Hall in December 1861. The new hospital had a total of forty-four beds, consisting of two large general wards of fourteen beds each, two smaller fever wards of six beds each, and one special ward of four beds. At that time the hospital directors were appealing to the public to donate clothes for the children 'who frequently enter hospital in rags so worn and filthy as to be unfit for further use'. The irony of the situation was not lost on the author Dinah Craik, who observed the

> picturesque, historical, melancholy, noisome and abominable Old Town of Edinburgh, and not far away, the more healthful region known as 'The Meadows'. A pleasant place where there is green grass, and where the Edinburgh Volunteers come to do their rifle shooting of mornings, and where the genteel nursemaids from George Square or Buccleuch Place walk with their young charges, and the un-genteel youthful fry from Morningside come out to play, barefooted and rough-headed. But the children of the lower class still abiding in the tall 'lands' twelve storeys high, the dark cellars, the wynds and closes so foul that the only cleansing would be a good wholesome fire like the Great Fire of London. Alas, the children who live there never come near The Meadows unless the angel of sickness, and it is an angel then, carries them away to lie clean and quiet in a peaceful, tiny crib in one of the wards at Meadowside House. It is more like a family home than a hospital and its very simplicity and plainness are a great charm.

The most serious group of ailments was the infectious diseases which were treated at Meadowside House up until 1885 when the City Fever Hospital was established in the Old Infirmary building in Infirmary Street. The Sick Children's Report for 1865 stated that 165 fever cases were admitted, of which 57 were typhus, 35 'febricula', 24 typhoid, 28 scarlatina, and 21 measles. Although these proportions varied from year to year, typhoid, typhus and scarlatina were predominant, whereas diphtheria was not nearly so common. Typhoid was a major problem. It progressed from 11 cases in 1862 to 48 in 1878, with 3 deaths. There was a serious recurrence among the staff in 1890, resulting in the death of one nurse. This outbreak was seen as particularly serious as fever cases had not been admitted to the hospital since 1885 when the new fever hospital opened. An intensive inspection of Meadowside House did not reveal any cause for concern but nevertheless the directors took the precaution of moving the patients and staff out to temporary accommodation at Plewlands House in Morningside. A further lengthy examination of Meadowside House revealed nothing to explain the outbreak but at least it gave the directors time to consider the future development of the hospital. As Plewlands was considered to be too remote from the main centres of population in Edinburgh, an idea was put forward to demolish Meadowside House and replace it with a much larger modern building. However, when it was discovered that the Royal Infirmary also wished to expand, Meadowside House was abandoned in favour of yet another site — this time on the south side of the Meadows — at Rillbank, then occupied by the Trades Maiden Hospital.

Although Rillbank was an ideal site for the new hospital, the existing building had to be demolished as it was completely unsuited to redevelopment or extension. Plans for a new hospital, costing £40,000, to accommodate 118 patients were drawn by the architect George Washington Browne. Despite the huge capital costs it was the directors' greatest wish that the hospital continue to be privately funded. Fortunately a substantial donation of £10,000 (previously intended to upgrade Meadowside House) was given by Lady Jane Dundas in memory of her sister Lady Caroline Charteris. This was later increased by a further gift of £1,500 to meet the additional cost of the new wing. The completed building incorporated a sculptured stone on the outside wall of the west wing to commemorate this generous donation:

THE LADY CAROLINE CHARTERIS WING, ERECTED IN
LOVING MEMORY OF A BEAUTIFUL AND BENEFICENT
LIFE BY HER SISTER LADY JANE DUNDAS

The hospital was constructed of red Corsehill sandstone on a south-facing site. The basic ground plan is E-shaped with the central projecting administrative block linked by corridors to the east and west wings. The central doorway is heavily sculptured between two pillars of alternate square and round courses, and above the inner door lintel are written the words:

IN AS MUCH AS YE HAVE DONE IT UNTO ONE OF
THE LEAST OF THESE YE HAVE DONE IT UNTO ME

The identical, three-storey wings have twin octagonal towers, between which open verandahs were constructed, but later enclosed. The administrative block housed the surgical theatre, the medical lecture room and the Directors' Board Room. Each wing contained two principal wards located on the ground and first floors, spare wards and isolation units on the second floor, and kitchen and stores on the third floor.

One of the most interesting features is the tiny mortuary chapel located to the rear of the main building. It is lined with paintings done by Phoebe Traquair in 1885, which were originally at Meadowside House but were reinstated at Sciennes by the artist in 1895. A timber dado runs round all four walls, above which are life-sized angels against a backcloth of horizontal bands representing the six days of creation. At the north end there is a panel 'Maternity' and at the south end 'The Cup of Life' and 'The Bridge of Life'.

The Out-Patients' Department, entered from Sylvan Place, was erected in 1903. It was also designed by Browne but built in grey stone some of which is believed to have come from the demolished Rillbank House.

Most of the building was completed in time for the official opening on 31st October 1895, an event which attracted detailed coverage by *The Scotsman* on the following day. The ceremony was performed by Her Royal Highness Princess Beatrice in the Bathgate Ward in the presence of Lord Provost MacDonald and many other dignitaries. One of the wards was named after Princess Beatrice and the entire west wing after Lady Caroline Charteris. While making a tour of the building the Princess presented to each of the nurses a silver commemorative badge gifted by the four physicians, Drs Carmichael, Playfair, Burn Murdoch and Joseph Bell.

Since its formation, the Hospital has been in the forefront of several new developments in the treatment of child ailments. Initially there were no specific arrangements for surgical treatment, the surgeon of the day taking it in turn to act as consulting surgeon. However, when fever cases were no longer admitted, there were spare beds available, and on 1st November 1887 a Surgical Ward was opened at Meadowside House under the charge of Mr Joseph Bell, President of the Royal College of Surgeons. The ward grew quickly in size and influence, 1222 surgical cases being treated in 1895. When Joseph Bell resigned in 1897 to become Consulting Surgeon he was succeeded by another very eminent surgeon Mr Harold J. Stiles (later Sir Harold), who held the position for another twenty-three years. Shortly after Mr Stiles' appointment an additional surgical ward, the Mackay-Smith Ward, was opened, increasing the number of cots to forty. The resultant increase in surgical work meant that the medical theatre on the first floor had to be converted to a new operating theatre.

A modest Department of two cots for Diseases of the Ear, Nose and Throat in Childhood was also established in 1913 under the charge of Dr W. G. Porter. Unfortunately his pioneering work was curtailed when he died in action in 1917 whilst serving as a Major in the Royal Artillery. His work was continued by Dr Douglas Guthrie, leading to the creation of the Meikleham Ward of twelve cots. A related aspect of the work was given separate recognition in 1932 when a Clinic for Disorders of Speech was set up as a branch of the Ear, Nose and Throat Department. This Clinic later became a centre for the instruction of students from the Edinburgh School of Speech Therapy.

From the very beginning the Hospital was committed to the study of child diseases and the dissemination of that knowledge to students of medicine. These aims, which were secondary only to the treatment of patients, were contained in the promoters' resolution dated 5th May 1859: 'To promote the advancement of medical science with reference to the diseases of childhood, and especially to provide for the more efficient instruction of students in this department of knowledge'. A system of clinical teaching was established in 1860, greatly strengthened in 1865 by the introduction of a course of lectures for advanced students. These were usually conducted in the wards where practical demonstration was available. Of particular relevance was a series of lectures in 1876 by Dr Peel Ritchie on the Medical Diseases and Management of Children. Clinical teaching was greatly reduced during the Hospital's temporary residence at Plewlands in view of the lengthy travelling time for students.

When the new hospital at Sciennes opened in 1895 paediatrics was not regarded as a separate branch of medicine: indeed it had always been linked, in a somewhat secondary role, to midwifery and gynaecology. However, attitudes were changing, influenced principally by the work done by John Thomson, author, in 1898, of *The Clinical*

Study and Treatment of Sick Children. This led in the early years of the twentieth century to many graduates being attracted from other parts of the world to attend special postgraduate courses. This immense build-up of interest in teaching was rewarded in 1931 by the foundation of the Edward Clark Chair of Child Life and Health at Edinburgh University. This was the first such chair in the United Kingdom to include the wider study of the child *in health* as well as disease, all preceding chairs having been confined to diseases of children. Its first Professor was Dr Charles McNeil, Physician to the Hospital since 1920 whose pioneering work made a significant contribution to neo-natal paediatrics, paediatric neurology and cardiology, as well as to the preventive and social aspects of child life.

Over the last few decades several important changes have taken place to maintain the hospital in the forefront of child medicine. As properties were acquired in Rillbank Terrace and Millerfield Place, various administrative functions were transferred from the main hospital building. Nos. 16, 17 and 25 Hatton Place have also been acquired for the Department of Child Life and Health but any further development, or change of use of premises, to the south of Sciennes Road has met with serious opposition from various local amenity groups. In April 1985 a new Haematology Department in Millerfield Place was opened by Princess Alexandra, and in October 1985 a new Casualty Department was opened on the east corner of Sylvan Place and Sciennes Road. Above the Casualty Department a new Neurology Ward was opened in October 1989. The complement of beds under the control of the hospital is around 238, some of . these being at other locations, namely Forteviot House in Hope Terrace, the Astley Ainslie Hospital, and Douglas House in Lauder Road. The main hospital has seven wards dealing with their own group of diseases: Ward 1, cancers, respiratory and cardiac problems; Ward 2, endocrine diseases and neurology relating to older child patients; Ward 3, plastic surgery involving congenital defects and burns; Ward 4, general surgery, neo-natal surgery and cardiac surgery; Ward 5, neurology and gastroenterology; Ward 6, ear, nose and throat; Ward 7, neurology.

Recent advances in surgical and medical treatment have resulted in a very different patient-duration profile. Emphasis on community care has meant that young patients are hospitalised for a much shorter time than previously. Modern life-support systems and new surgical techniques now facilitate the care of seriously ill children who in past years would have died. This, in turn, has put greater strain on the need to maintain intensive-care nursing in several locations throughout the building. It is hoped that, well within the next decade, a purpose-built extension to the north of the existing building will allow a concentration of services in one area, making the best use of trained staff.

The Royal Edinburgh Hospital for Sick Children continues to deal with patients from all parts of the country and is the leading teaching hospital in Scotland for child ailments.

LONGMORE HOSPITAL

THE EDINBURGH HOSPITAL FOR INCURABLES was founded in 1874 as the outcome of a scheme for providing a single central hospital for incurable patients throughout Scotland. Whilst the existence of such a hospital was generally welcomed by the medical profession, several eminent doctors, among them Lord Lister, Robert Christison, Douglas Maclagan, William Turner Argyll Robertson, Thomas Keith, Matthews Duncan and Joseph Bell voiced the opinion that several smaller hospitals would be preferable, near where the patients' relatives lived. The merits and demerits of the scheme were discussed at length at a public meeting in the Freemasons' Hall in George Street on 1st December 1874, as a result of which the Edinburgh Association for Incurables was formed. Their first task was to raise sufficient funds to set up the first hospital. A successful bazaar was held which

Queen Mary accompanied by Lady Pentland at the gates of the Longmore Hospital in Salisbury Place on 18th July 1911. Courtesy of Longmore Hospital.

raised £5,000, most of which was used to purchase, renovate and furnish a former dwelling house at No. 8 Salisbury Place. The new hospital, open to incurably ill patients throughout the country, was ready by 1875, but within a very short time, there was a long waiting list. Fortunately, help was again at hand.

At the Annual General Meeting of the Edinburgh Association for Incurables on 13th February 1877 an announcement was made that a substantial gift would be made by the Trustees of the late John Alexander Longmore of Deanshaugh. J. A. Longmore W.S., the only son of Adam Longmore, Junior, of the Exchequer, was born on 28th October 1812 and died, unmarried, on 16th April 1875. By the terms of his will, his Trustees were empowered to grant a gift of £10,000 provided the Hospital 'should supply accommodation for incurable patients of all classes and at the same time commemorate Mr Longmore's munificent bequest for the relief of such sufferers'. This substantial sum of money allowed the directors to purchase, in 1877, the adjacent properties of Nos. 9 and 10 Salisbury Place. No. 9 was occupied as the Cripples Home under the control of its matron, Miss Barrowman, and No. 10 was the house of George Lawson of George Lawson & Son, bakers and confectioners, who had retail premises at West Newington, Lothian Street and Earl Grey Street. Plans were prepared for a new hospital by the architects, Kinnear and Peddie, but building did not start until the end of 1878. One of the early difficulties was to find alternative accommodation for the existing patients. The first proposal was to build the hospital in two halves and transfer the patients when the first half was completed, but the idea was abandoned in view of the potential danger and discomfort caused by being too near to the building site. Shortly thereafter, two suitable houses were located at Fisherrow and fitted out for the sum of £217 9s 5d, enabling the fifteen remaining patients to transfer there, early in June 1879. The completed hospital, with accommodation for fifty beds, was opened on 10th December 1880 by Sir Thomas Jamieson Boyd, Lord Provost of Edinburgh. It consisted of a centre three-storey block, flanked by two wings of two storeys with a total frontage of one hundred and sixty feet, and a depth of one hundred and eighty feet. The acquisition of the ground had cost £6,000 and the completed building a further £14,000. Over the entrance was a pediment with an inscription which fulfilled the provisions of the Longmore bequest, but hardly gave the inmates cause to believe that they would benefit from any advances in medical science: THE ASSOCIATION FOR INCURABLES LONGMORE HOSPITAL. The patients' register, opened on 27th March 1884, shows patients from Edinburgh, North Berwick, Glenshee, Methil and Dumfries, among whom were several teenagers and a few children.

Despite the nature of the illnesses, progressive muscular atrophy, paraplegia, spinal sclerosis, rachitis, spina bifida and tuberculosis, some patients were resident at Longmore for a remarkably long time, due, no doubt, to the expert care and attention provided by the staff. An early report on the hospital stated that the number of patients was initially restricted to twenty-five, some of whom were 'paying patients', and that all the wards were fitted with Manchester open fireplaces. By 1886 the demand for accommodation was again acute, necessitating the purchase of a further two adjacent houses which were converted to provide another fourteen beds.

On 5th November 1886 the hospital received one of many Royal visitors, Her Majesty Queen Victoria, who presented engraved portraits of herself for each ward, consented to be Patron of the Association, and donated £50 to the funds. A new wing for an additional thirty-six beds was constructed on the site of the 1880 annexe and opened on 3rd October 1893 by the Duke and Duchess of York, who signed the visitors' book simply as 'George' and 'Victoria Mary'. In 1898 the total accommodation was increased to one hundred and fifty beds by the erection of the west wing, provided especially for the treatment of tuberculosis and cancer, which was opened on 5th January 1899 by Her Grace the Duchess of Buccleuch. In 1903 the hospital became The Royal Edinburgh Hospital for Incurables, incorporated by Royal Charter.

In the early days, most of the staff resided in the hospital but in 1938 a report was submitted on the possibility of acquiring Nos. 9 and 11 Salisbury Road for the construction of a new home for the nursing staff. The two houses were demolished and a new five-storey building, designed by J. Douglas Miller, was erected, providing accommodation for seventy nurses. After some delay at the beginning of the Second World War, the building was completed at a cost of £40,000.

At Salisbury Place the west wing was reconstructed to

include a theatre and radiological department and the large wards were divided into smaller units to provide more privacy for patients. The new complex was opened by the Duchess of Gloucester on 1st October 1954.

St. Raphael's

IN 1877, BLACKFORD AVENUE, as the name suggests, was a long, narrow, tree-lined road giving access to Blackford House, to the south of Grange Loan. At the Grange Loan end there were three large detached houses: West Grange was on the east corner of Blackford Avenue and Grange Loan; Ashfield, later the home of the Trades Maiden Hospital, was on the west corner; and Dunard, later occupied by Grange Home School, lay between Ashfield and Kilgraston Road. Many of the streets in the south part of the Grange were formed, but there was very little development other than at Fountainhall Road. On its west section, later renamed Grange Terrace, South Park had just been built, and terraced houses were beginning to appear on the north side.

Such was the early development of this part of the Grange when Hugh Rose Jnr. acquired an extensive feu on the north corner of Blackford Avenue and South Oswald Road. Hugh Rose Jnr. was the eldest son of Hugh Rose, the founder of the firm, Craig and Rose, 'oil merchants, drysalters, oil boilers, paint, colour and varnish manufacturers' of 172 Leith Walk. The house at Blackford Avenue, designed by David MacGibbon, was named Kilravock after Kilravock Castle near Nairn, the home of the Rose Clan, where Hugh Rose Jnr. had lived before coming to Edinburgh. Hugh Rose remained at Kilravock, in Blackford Avenue, until around 1900 when the extensive, turreted mansion and stables were sold to George Balfour Turnbull, an Edinburgh stockbroker. Turnbull sold the property in 1911 to M. J. Lothian, whose interest in the house ceased some time during the First World War.

At the end of the First World War, Kilravock was

A group of patients and staff at the doorway of St. Raphael's Hospital probably shortly after the end of the First World War. Courtesy of the Little Company of Mary.

acquired by the Scottish Branch of the British Red Cross and Ministry of Pensions with the intention of setting up a home for severely disabled ex-servicemen. The project was organised by a committee under the direction of Lady Anne Kerr, sister of the Duke of Norfolk, who invited the Sisters of the Little Company of Mary to make preparations to receive the first patients. The house was renamed St. Raphael's after St. Raphael the Angel of Healing, and in commemoration of Lady Anne's husband, Major-General Lord Ralph Kerr, who was killed in action in 1916. The hospital, staffed by six sisters, received its first patients in 1919 — thirty-three casualties from the battlefields of Europe, the first patient being a thirty-one year-old officer described, rather succinctly, in the hospital journal as a 'paralysed and incurable Protestant'. Despite the traumatic circumstances, a relatively cheerful atmosphere was maintained between the patients and the staff, who were given great encouragement from the many visitors, including King George and Queen Mary, Earl

Haig, Cardinal Bourne, Father Martindale and Lady Dick Lauder of Grange House.

A detailed history of St. Raphael's is contained in the Edinburgh section of *Place of Springs*, by Mary Campion, which records the first hundred years of the Province of the Maternal Heart of the Little Company of Mary founded in 1877. At the end of the first decade at St. Raphael's the number of war victims was greatly reduced and the hospital began to receive its first civilian patients. The Little Company of Mary acquired the hospital from the Red Cross, built St. David's Ward in memory of Lady Anne's son, who was also killed in the First World War, and opened the first female ward in 1929. In the early 1930s the need for further expansion was evident, as a result of which a new wing was built and opened in 1934 by Archbishop Andrew J. McDonald of St. Andrews and Edinburgh. At the outbreak of the Second World War the hospital braced itself again to receive war casualties, but this time the patients were elderly civilians who had lost their homes during the London blitz. In 1948 the hospital opted to remain outwith the National Health Service. The last link with the original home was severed as late as 1958 when Dan Collins died, the only remaining patient from the First World War.

In 1965 a major building programme was undertaken to provide twenty-four bedrooms and a small ward for children. Arrangements for geriatric patients were greatly improved and nine beds were provided for elderly female patients. A few years later, in June 1969, the Golden Jubilee celebrations were kept to a modest scale in view of world poverty, the funds raised being gifted to the Third World. At the time of the centenary of the Little Company of Mary in 1977, St. Raphael's remained the only Catholic general hospital in the East of Scotland, with forty-three beds, and seventeen sisters under the direction of Sister Superior Genevieve Begadon.

In 1982 St. Raphael's entered another phase in its long development when a decision was taken not to continue as a small general hospital. Following discussion between the Little Company of Mary and Viewpoint Housing Association

The Community of the Little Company of Mary in 1950 at the entrance to the 1934 extension to St. Raphael's Hospital. Courtesy of the Little Company of Mary.

Limited the St. Raphael's Housing Association Limited was formed to take over the hospital and to convert it into a Nursing Home for the long-term care of the frail elderly. Substantial funds were expended on the adaptation of the buildings and a more domestic environment was provided. The new unit successfully provides a wide range of care for over forty elderly people of both sexes. Further improvements in the facilities are also planned without materially increasing the number of residents. The old name of Kilravock has also been revived with the formation of the Kilravock Housing Association Limited which completed a co-ownership sheltered housing development in the grounds to the north in 1989.

ROYAL DICK VETERINARY COLLEGE

THE HANDSOME NEO-CLASSICAL BUILDING at Summerhall, facing west along Melville Drive, is known by most citizens of

Edinburgh as the home of the Royal Dick Veterinary College. It was built on the site of Bryson's brewery in 1914, at which time veterinary medicine in Edinburgh had been established for almost a century. Since the Summerhall building was opened the college has expanded to house various new departments, few of which were envisaged when the idea of a veterinary school was first considered in the late eighteenth century.

Several veterinary schools were established on the Continent before 1800, the earliest of which was at Lyons in 1762. This was followed by a similar school at Turin in 1769 and one at Dresden in 1774. In fact, most European countries had established veterinary schools before the London School was established in 1791. Tentative discussions took place in Edinburgh around 1793 but nothing came of the proposals until more than a quarter of a century later. Although Edinburgh (and indeed Scotland) did not have its own school until 1823, several pioneers had emigrated earlier to set up, or administer, veterinary schools in Canada, Australia and America. In Edinburgh the early history and subsequent development of veterinary education was almost exclusively the province of the Dick family.

In the *History of the Edinburgh Veterinary College* O. Charnock Bradley records that John Dick and his wife Jean Anderson are said to have come to Edinburgh from Aberdeenshire when 'they were both about eighteen years of age'. Charnock Bradley, however, highlights the obvious ambiguity of this statement by pointing out that John Dick was four years younger than his wife. On the assumption that it was John who was eighteen, the year was 1787. One of their first houses in Edinburgh was at White Horse Close in the Canongate, but it is not known how long they lived there. They were at Rose Street in April 1799 and within a few months had moved to what was later known as Nottingham Place (to the east of Leith Street). The *Edinburgh and Leith Post Office Directory* contains the entry 'John

The chimney of Bryson's Brewery at Summerhall was demolished and the site cleared for the construction of the new Royal Dick Veterinary College in 1914. Courtesy of the Faculty of Veterinary Medicine, University of Edinburgh.

Dick, smith, Nottingham Place' from 1805 to the 1814-15 issue, and from 1815 the entry is 'Dick, John smith and farrier, 15 Clyde Street'.

John and Jean Dick had eight children of whom only two survived to adulthood, namely, Mary born in 1791, and William born in 1793: four other children died in infancy; one was stillborn; and John, born in 1802, died prematurely at the age of nineteen. Despite such tragic losses, which were probably no worse than those suffered by many other families of the time, William and Mary eventually succeeded in bringing the family name to the forefront of veterinary education. When William Dick was born on 6th May 1793 the family was probably living at White Horse Close. He was educated at a school run by the Rev. J. Robinson in Paul's Works and later at Mr Kesson's school in Shakespeare Square. After school he worked closely with his father in the farrier's business but also continued his formal education by studying rhetoric and mathematics. His determination to bridge the enormous gap between a skilled farrier and a veterinary surgeon led him to attend numerous lectures, notably those of Dr John Barclay of Surgeons' Square, the leading anatomist, a Director of the Highland Society.

Gradually Dick began to prepare himself for qualification as a veterinary surgeon: in 1817 he went to London where he attended Camden Town School to hear lectures on diseases of the horse by Professor Coleman. He obtained his diploma in veterinary surgery on 27th January 1818, and returned to Edinburgh eager to put into practice his new-found knowledge. Under the auspices of a Mr Scott he advertised, in the autumn, a series of lectures on veterinary surgery, but unfortunately no-one attended. Daunted, but appearing not to be, Dick offered the same series in 1819-20, when he attracted four pupils, only one of whom attended regularly. On the premise that one is better than none, Dick rented the Calton Convening Rooms for the following session when the attendance rose to nine pupils. Surely the idea was by then beginning to show some appeal. By a fortunate coincidence the School of Arts was established in 1821 at the

Freemasons' Hall in Niddry Street, which gave Dick a useful platform on which to gain experience as a lecturer. For two consecutive sessions he offered to give veterinary lectures free, which were attended in the first year by seventeen pupils. It was not until 1823, however, that he made the breakthrough for which he had been planning for so long. On 15th July 1823 Dick was appointed lecturer in veterinary science at the Highland Society Veterinary School. In the first session he delivered forty-six lectures to twenty-five students producing a total revenue of £42 from fees, and £50 as a grant from the Highland Society. Lectures were held at the Calton Convening Rooms until 1829 when they were transferred to the Clyde Street premises. Excerpts from a description of the premises confirm that the early veterinary school was essentially a practical business:

> You may fancy to yourself a room of no very great dimensions in an old and apparently long untenanted house in Clyde Street. You enter it from the street door, and are immediately struck with the delightful confusion which seems to reign within. Skeletons of all descriptions . . . from a horse to an ape, not ranged in 'regular order all of a row,' but standing higgelty-piggelty, their ranks having been broken by the Professor's table, and their heads looking in all directions, as if thrown together by chance. Over the Professor's 'devoted head' is seen suspended a portion of inflated and injected intestine, with its mesenteric expansion dangling in the air, something like a lure for flies; whilst all around the room, and especially in the corners, are heaped together vast quantities of diseased bones, and other preparations, seemingly without order, and without arrangement . . .

In 1833 new buildings were opened at Clyde Street consisting of a lecture room, museum, dissecting room, infirmary and forge. The entire cost of £2,500 was met by Dick with a grant of £50 from the Highland Society towards the cost of fitting out the lecture room. When the new building opened there were fifty students, increasing gradually to over one hundred by 1839, the year in which the titles 'College' and 'Professor' were conferred.

As the Edinburgh school increased its reputation to at least that of the Royal Veterinary College of London, a proposal was put forward to create one unified profession. On 8th March 1844 the Royal College of Veterinary Surgeons was created by Royal Charter incorporating the members of the Royal Veterinary College of London and the Veterinary College of Edinburgh. The schools remained separate, independent and unconnected. On election to the Council Dick signed the Charter, although it must have been evident to him that the work done by the new body would encroach on the work already being done by the Highland and Agricultural Society. The potential for further friction lay ahead. The first examinations of the Royal College, held in Edinburgh in April 1844, were monitored by a deputation from London, whose report contained some very derogatory remarks on the standard of the papers set. Dick was particularly incensed by one section of the report which alleged 'that there was no examination on Chemistry, none on Materia Medica, none on Physiology, and none on the diseases of cattle that deserved the name'. In protest, the Highland and Agricultural Society ceased to hold its own examinations, but these were reintroduced in 1848. Many years later in 1879 when holders of the Highland and Agricultural Society certificates were admitted to the Royal College, the Society agreed not to hold veterinary examinations after April 1881.

Dick died on 4th April 1866 at the age of seventy-two, having devoted the whole of his life to establishing the veterinary profession in Scotland. He was buried in New Calton Burial Ground only a few hundred yards from the Calton Convening Rooms where, forty-five years previously, he had made his first faltering steps into the world of veterinary education. Charnock Bradley wrote that when Dick first thought of establishing a veterinary school in Edinburgh, there were fewer than a dozen veterinary

William Dick, founder of the Edinburgh Veterinary College which later bore his name. From *History of the Edinburgh Veterinary College*.

practitioners in the whole of Scotland and 'at that time, the treatment of sick animals was, in the main, in the hands of those with no better claim to the office than that conferred upon them by a superb effrontery and self-assurance cloaking profound and gross ignorance'. That the profession had rid itself of quacks and charlatans was clearly evidenced by the obituary notices which appeared in the national press and professional journals. Dick had been a man of the highest professional standing, a strict disciplinarian, and possessed of an unnerving blend of sarcasm, ridicule, praise and encouragement. In addition to his lifelong service to veterinary science he was a member of the Royal Physical Society of Edinburgh, Deacon of the Hammermen, Dean of Guild, Moderator of the High Constables and a member of the Town Council. Despite his many official appointments he was also a great supporter of Heriot's Hospital and Morningside Lunatic Asylum. Perhaps some idea of the 'inner man' can be gauged from the following extract of the obituary which appeared in *The Scotsman* for 6th April 1866:

> Mr Dick was a man of strong natural abilities and in his own profession of great acquirements and experience. In political and ecclesiastical matters his views were somewhat extreme and always expressed with no reserve and some roughness. He did not know fear and had neither time nor skill for the mincing of words. But he was so honest, so truthful, so good-natured and so free from self-seeking that he had almost no enemies and hearty friends everywhere. The figure and the name of 'Willie Dick' were long and conspicuously among us and for long too he will be missed and mourned.

After the death of Dick the Veterinary College of Edinburgh faced a very uncertain future. Many of the heads of department and lecturers had been with Dick for many years and had helped him to formulate the character of the college. Dick remained a bachelor all his days, but he was survived by Mary, his elder sister, who had spent much of her time in support of her brother's ideals. She was a most businesslike woman — austere and calvinistic by nature — but when

Mary Dick, elder sister of William Dick, austere and Calvinistic by nature, and in many ways 'the power behind the throne'. From *History of the Edinburgh Veterinary College*.

Dick died she was seventy-four years of age and not likely to maintain a high profile in the new organisation. She removed from Clyde Street, where the family had lived since 1815, and retired to Burntisland. For many years after, she kept in close contact with the Trustees and the Principal of the

College, until her death on 14th July 1883 at the age of ninety-two. She was buried beside her brother in New Calton Burial Ground.

By the terms of his will, Dick left his entire estate for the continuation of the college, to be administered by the Lord Provost, Magistrates and Council of the City of Edinburgh as Trustees. They appointed a new Principal, J. H. B. Hallen, but he remained in the post for less than a year. His replacement, William Williams M.R.C.V.S., was welcomed by Mary Dick, who recalled that he had been one of her brother's ablest pupils. Unfortunately his time as Principal was beset with problems which shook the very foundations of the college. Thomas Strangeways, Professor of Anatomy since 1856, died in February 1869 and his successor William C. Branford had his appointment cancelled in November 1870. When Dr George A. Davidson, Professor of Anatomy, died in 1873 the department was once again thrown into confusion: his successor, Dr John Murie, found himself at the centre of discord between himself, the students and Principal Williams. This time the consequences were more serious than even Dick could have foreseen. A Minute of the Committee of Management dated 15th July 1873 asked Principal Williams to resign before the beginning of the winter session began. He promptly did so, and left Clyde Street, taking with him (apparently legitimately) over forty students, most of the clinical material for instruction, and the college library. He set up a rival organisation, the New Veterinary College, at Gayfield House in East London Street, leaving only nine pupils at the original college. Within seven years of his death, Dick's life's work lay in ruins, pillaged by one of his own pupils, whilst Mary could only look on in helpless anger.

The Trustees began again. On 26th August 1873 they appointed William Fearnley as Principal with the rather daunting task of dealing with continued staff problems, very few students, scanty equipment and similar remuneration. Differences of opinion with Dr Murie soon surfaced. Murie

The neo-classical building of the Royal Dick Veterinary College at Summerhall designed by David McArthy. The memorial stone was laid by the Marquess of Linlithgow on 21st July 1914. From *History of the Edinburgh Veterinary College*.

resigned within a few months but the problem did not end there. After enduring constant interference from the Trustees, Fearnley also tendered his resignation with a letter which must be admired for its clinical assessment of the situation:

> Events are constantly occurring which render it painfully evident to me that I have neither your support nor confidence. This being so, I must either resign an anomalous office or lose my self-respect, and as I infinitely prefer to retain the latter I respectfully tender my resignation.

The college had suffered from one major setback after another in the years immediately after the death of Dick. Ironically, one of the few positive achievements during that time arose out of the existence of Williams' rival college. As Edinburgh then had two veterinary colleges, Mary Dick wrote to the Trustees suggesting that the identity of the original college would be better safeguarded if it were named 'The

Dick Veterinary College'. The Trustees agreed and in the following year 'Royal' was added to give the full title of the Royal Dick Veterinary College. Perhaps in deference to the new name, the college entered into a period of stability and gradual progress. Thomas Walley was appointed Principal in 1874 and remained in that position until 1894, when the number of students attending the college exceeded three hundred. When Thomas Walley died in 1894 the same 'quiet and unostentatious development' was continued by the new Principal, John Robert Urquhart Dewar.

In the early part of the twentieth century the college again entered a period of change. The Trustees agreed to transfer the management of the college to a new Board of Management in 1905 and a new Chair of Pathology and Bacteriology was endowed by Alexander Inglis Maccallum. The college became incorporated by Act of Parliament in 1906, and the University of Edinburgh obtained power to grant degrees in Veterinary Science, which were introduced in 1911. One of the main problems confronting the new Board was the provision of adequate premises. Clyde Street had been altered and extended on numerous occasions, and whilst it was first thought that modernisation would be sufficient, a report in February 1907 recommended the construction of a completely new building. After considerable delay the Summerhall site was purchased, the old buildings were demolished, and work started almost immediately. The memorial stone was laid by the Marquess of Linlithgow on 21st July 1914, and despite the intervention of the First World War, the building was sufficiently complete to allow classes to move from Clyde Street in 1916. A few relics of special significance were taken from the Clyde Street building to the new premises at Summerhall. Perhaps the best known was the figure of a horse which had adorned the highest point of the Clyde Street building. This was carefully dismantled and placed over a stone archway at the entrance to the new Maccallum Clinical Department. The bulky figure of Dick, sculpted by John Rhind in 1883, which had sat under the clock in the Clyde Street yard, was repositioned to look out over an ornamental garden in the quadrangle of the new building. The library of volumes, which had belonged to Dick personally, were incorporated in the College War Memorial.

The first of several extensions to the Summerhall premises was completed in 1937 in the form of an L-shaped, two-storey building to the south and east of the former Hope Park United Free Church. The handsome Gothic-spired church gradually fell into disrepair and was eventually demolished in 1949. In 1951 the college became a constituent part of Edinburgh University within the Faculty of Medicine and was designated the Royal (Dick) School of Veterinary Studies. Despite its growing importance and influence, it was not until 1966 that the Northumberland Committee (chaired by His Grace The Duke of Northumberland, K.G.), recommended substantial grants for new accommodation at Summerhall to house Veterinary Pathology, Microbiology, Biochemistry and a Small Animal Clinic. As a result the Tower was built on the north-west corner, almost exactly where Hope Park United Free Church had stood. This apparently functional building of little architectural merit, houses numerous laboratories and the Evelyn Head Lecture Theatre, gifted in 1971. The completed Tower, with panoramic views of Edinburgh from its upper storeys, was opened by the Duke of Northumberland on 7th February 1973 to mark the 150th anniversary of the college. In the same building programme a section of the original building on the south-east corner (previously used as a large animal operating theatre) was demolished and replaced with a modern brick building for the small animal clinic. As demolition included the stone archway supporting the Clyde Street horse it was decided to transfer it to the roof of the new building. Unfortunately, owing to the weight-bearing capabilities of the new roof the horse was positioned with its head turned away from the natural angle of vision. Whether this signifies that the poor beast has turned its back on any further moves, or is perhaps looking out over the rooftops to pastures new, is a matter of conjecture. Finally in 1985 Hope Park and Buccleuch Congregational Church to the east of the 1937 extension was acquired and tastefully converted into tutorial and laboratory accommodation, and a refectory.

In addition to the Summerhall premises the college has an extensive presence on two hundred acres of ground at the Bush Estate near Penicuik. This was established as a Field Station in 1962 to provide facilities for farm animal clinical work and animal husbandry. Bush Estate was also recommended by the Riley Report of 1989 as the site of a new integrated veterinary school for the whole of Scotland. Whilst such a school would undoubtedly give greater stability on account of its size, the Riley Report envisaged the closure of both the Glasgow and Edinburgh colleges in their present form. These proposals have proved to be very controversial, and, at the time of writing, no decision has been reached.

CHAPTER 9

THE CHANGING FACE
OF SCIENNES
AND THE GRANGE

HAVING CONSIDERED THE HISTORY AND DEVELOPMENT OF THE CHURCHES, the schools and the hospitals, there is one last group which has made a significant impact on both Sciennes and the Grange, in varying degrees over the last century. Sciennes has always had an interesting mix of private dwellings, small businesses and one or two larger firms of national or international importance. On the other hand, the Grange was laid out as an exclusively residential development on which no businesses were permitted. In some ways the trend has been reversed in recent years, with Causewayside and Sciennes losing many of their traditional firms, and the sites being developed for housing. A quadrangle of flats was built in 1986 on the site of St. Katherine's Works in Sciennes, previously occupied by Bertrams, manufacturers of papermaking machinery, and the building occupied by Neill & Co., the printers, in Causewayside has been redeveloped as flats.

The position in the Grange is slightly more complicated in that the presence of businesses or institutions in a largely residential area is not immediately evident. Nevertheless, several larger buildings, originally used as private dwellings, have been acquired for non-residential use, whilst others have been bought by organisations specialising in residential care.

WEST GRANGE ARTESIAN WELL

WEST GRANGE lay immediately to the east of the junction of Blackford Avenue and Grange Loan. Later it was enclosed on the east side by St. Thomas Road and on the south side by the back gardens of the houses on the north side of Grange Terrace. The name, West Grange, appears on very early maps, presumably when the dwelling house was of fairly modest proportions but it was extended and renovated on numerous occasions over the years. There is some doubt as to whether West Grange was owned by Henry J. Younger in the 1880s when part of the garden ground was used to sink a well for William Younger & Co. Ltd., the famous Edinburgh brewers. West Grange was occupied by a Mrs Smith from 1860 to 1887, after which it became vacant. In 1887 Henry J. Younger was living at Ashfield, a large detached property to the west of Blackford Avenue, once the home of David MacGibbon, the architect. Around the same time (1887) Younger & Co were looking for a site to sink a well, which according to *The Younger Centuries* 'was duly found beside Mr Henry's own house'. The use of the word 'beside' would more accurately describe West Grange than Ashfield. In addition, when the various wells were sunk adjacent to the garden ground of West Grange, no objection was raised by the owner or occupier of that house, which would perhaps suggest that the owner of West Grange was Younger himself.

In September 1889 William Younger & Co. Ltd., of Horse Wynd and Holyrood Breweries, applied to the Dean of Guild Court for permission 'to sink a Well, erect Engine House, Houses and Tank at Grange Loan', to augment the supply of spring water for their brewing business at Holyrood. A complaint was received from a Miss Grant, who owned land to the east of the proposed site, but who lived at West Thorn in Lauder Road (now Douglas House, part of the Royal Hospital for Sick Children). Miss Grant wrote to the Court stating that:

Aerial view of West Grange 1950, looking east with Blackford Avenue at the bottom of the picture and Grange Loan at right angles to it. West Grange, with the circular driveway, and the Artesian Well lie on the south side of Grange Loan opposite Carlton Cricket Ground. Courtesy of Scottish and Newcastle Breweries P.L.C. and Scottish Brewing Archive.

> [The] district is one in which the houses are all of the villa class or of a class equivalent to villas and . . . the erection of an engine house and dwelling houses of the kind proposed would greatly injure the amenity of the respondent's property and diminish its value.

She later withdrew her objection and the work went ahead, resulting in a handsome, square stone block with a pitched slated roof. The ground floor contained the parlour and kitchen and the engine room to the rear, and the first and second floors were occupied as private dwellings for employees. Also on the second floor, at the highest possible level, was the water storage tank, which measured 25'4" ×

24'1" × 6', held 22,300 gallons and weighed 118 tons. A much grander scheme was introduced in December 1904 when William Younger & Co. Ltd. applied for permission to heighten the walls of the Well House, install a much larger tank, supported on square brick piers, and build a new engine house. The private living accommodation was also improved and a range of stables, coach house and harness room was built facing onto Grange Loan. The shaft of the well, eight feet in diameter, was sunk to a depth of two hundred feet. The rest water level (the natural level without pumping) varied between seventy-four feet and one hundred and two feet from the surface in winter, and dropped to between one hundred and eighty feet and one hundred and ninety-eight feet in summer. The water was pumped to the surface by two 3-stroke engines each with a capacity of 16,812 gallons per hour.

Within a hundred yards of the main tank in Grange Loan two other wells were sunk and later bored to a greater depth. The original petition was dated 5th May 1898 'to erect a Temporary House for the sinking of a well at West Grange, Blackford Avenue, Edinburgh, constructed with walls, partly stone, partly brick, timber and slated roof'. No official objections were received from neighbours, but the Court warned that 'the sinking of a well in proximity to so many dwelling houses will, owing to blasting operations, constitute a serious nuisance . . . and the old drain must be reconstructed with metal pipes'. The three wells were later interconnected to provide a constant supply of water to the overhead tank. From there the water, or liquor as it is referred to in the trade, ran by gravity in two separate pipes to the Holyrood and Abbey Breweries. The water flowed under Findhorn Place, Minto Street, Dalkeith Road (at the end of Blacket Avenue) and into Holyrood Park to the breweries. The second, older pipe took a different course towards the end of its journey and ran under Dumbiedykes.

The wells continued to supply water to the breweries until 1985, when Scottish and Newcastle Breweries discontinued their use of the supply. The well was capped, the machinery was removed, and the distinctive tank house with the square, harled pillars was demolished. The land was sold, and subsequently bought by Applecross Properties Ltd., who have constructed seven flats of various sizes in a three-storey building with mock balconies and a steeply pitched slated roof containing pedimented dormers.

The house known as West Grange was demolished prior to construction of a much larger block of flats in 1977. A tiny lodge house, with overhanging roof timbers, protruded into the roadway at the junction of Blackford Avenue and Grange Loan, until it was demolished in road improvement work in the 1960s.

BANK OF SCOTLAND

ON THE NORTH SIDE OF ST. ALBAN'S ROAD, three very similar detached properties, Nos. 58, 60 and 62, have been occupied by the Training and Management Development Department of the Bank of Scotland since 1974. Each building dates from around 1880 when the feus were allocated in accordance with Raeburn's Feuing Plan of 1877, referred to in Chapter 5.

The eastmost plot, on which No. 58 was built, was feued to William Barron on 1st November 1880. In 1883 he appears to have taken occupation of the completed house, Bellwood, although he also had property at Clifton House, Portobello. The house remained in private occupation until 1891, when it was taken over by Miss Cunningham, and used as Bellwood House Institution for the Education of Young Ladies until 1901. The name, Bellwood, was retained by subsequent private owners between 1903 and 1943, one of whom was J. Watson Alston, the manager of the London City Office of the Commercial Bank, whose Head Office was then at No. 14 George Street, Edinburgh. Mr Alston began his career with the Galashiels branch on 1st April 1899 and held several appointments in Edinburgh before going to London. In 1943 Bellwood again became a school, as the Preparatory Department of George Watson's Ladies College and the boys' school, George Watson's College.

The centre plot, on which No. 60 was built, was feued to James Brodie on 10th July 1880, but he does not appear to have occupied the house. The first recorded occupant, Major R. Greig, named the house 'Craigmichen', and lived there for more than thirty years. Craigmichen remained in private occupation until 1952, one of the last private owners being Raymond Hodgson of Raymond Hodgson & Co. Ltd., Knitwear, Wool and Hosiery Merchants of Blair Street. No. 60 was acquired by the Merchant Company Education Board from Lt.-Col. John Jeffrey Readman in May 1952.

The westmost plot, on which No. 62 was built (Monkton Lodge), was feued to Thomas Purvis on 11th March 1880, and remained in private occupation until 1955, when it was acquired by George Watson's College. The College continued at Nos. 58, 60 and 62 until 1974 when all three properties were sold by the Merchant Company Education Board to the Bank of Scotland. The Merchant Company acquired, in part exchange, the Bank's Training Centre at Tipperlinn Road, which backed onto George Watson's College ground in Colinton Road. This convenient arrangement allowed Watsons to use No. 9 as a boarding house for George Watson's College girls until 1984. At St. Alban's Road, the amenity ground on the south side of the road, which had previously been used as the school playing fields, was sold in 1974 to Viewpoint Housing Association for the construction of sheltered housing.

The three properties, forming the Bank's Training Department, are now interlinked, but the external stonework of the three original houses has not been significantly altered. No. 58 was built to the highest specification, with an imposing doorway, elegant staircases, and ornate plasterwork in the principal rooms. A large conservatory, at one time on the west wall, has been replaced by a modern single-storey extension linked to No. 60. The stained-glass staircase window of No. 58 contains the entwined initials W B and M H in the lower corners. On the assumption that the left-hand one reads W B and not B W, the initials are probably those of William Barron, the first owner, and his wife M H. The

The Artesian Well in Grange Loan was capped in 1985 and in 1990 the site was developed in a very distinctive style. Courtesy of Applecross Properties Ltd.

alternative explanation — that the initials are B W for Bellwood — appears less convincing. Both Nos. 60 and 62 have small stone-built wings on the east walls and No. 62 had a conservatory on the west wall. The date, 1881, is shown on an attractive staircase window at No. 62, which also has the original coachhouse, with a weather vane, to the rear of the property.

NATIONAL LIBRARY OF SCOTLAND

THE TALL, ANGULAR, STONE-CLAD, GLASS AND METAL BUILDING on the corner of Salisbury Place and Causewayside was built as an extension to the National Library of Scotland, and houses, among other departments, the Map Library and the Scottish Science Library. The origin of the National Library, however, precedes the Causewayside building by about three centuries.

The National Library of Scotland is a direct descendant of the Advocates' Library, which was inaugurated in 1689. From 1710 the Advocates' Library enjoyed the privilege of legal deposit, thus elevating it to the status of a national library, in practice, if not in name. In the 1920s, Sir Alexander Grant gifted a total of £200,000 to establish a National Library and provide for it a completely new building. Plans were drawn up, utilising the site on George IV Bridge, then occupied by the Sheriff Court. The National Library of Scotland was created by Act of Parliament in 1925, when the Advocates' Library gifted its substantial collection of books to the nation, retaining only the law library. Although construction of the new library, designed by Reginald Fairlie & Partners and built by Colin Macandrew and Partners Ltd., began in 1938, it was delayed during the War years and was not opened until 1956. In 1989 the National Library celebrated completion of its third century with a magnificent exhibition, *300 Years, 300 Books*, which included a rare and interesting deposit from each year since its formation in 1689.

Three main methods of acquisition – legal deposit, purchase and donation – have combined to produce a national depository of almost six million books, with the modern books arranged by size, not subject, on eighty-five miles of shelving from George IV Bridge down to the Cowgate. In addition to the published books there are 70,000 volumes of manuscripts, and 18,000 current newspapers and periodical titles. A recent innovation is the deposit of ephemeral material, which, taken collectively, provides a remarkable insight into many aspects of everyday life. Some of these items include knitting patterns, car manuals, theatre posters and children's comics. By contrast, the library's treasures include the last letter of Mary Queen of Scots, the Gutenberg Bible, Earl Haig's war diaries, and the most significant collections of Sir Walter Scott manuscripts in the world. With acquisitions increasing at the rate of 6,500 printed items every week the library has an almost insatiable appetite for space.

The tall angular towers of the National Library of Scotland at Causewayside, designed by Andrew Merrylees Associates, and built on the site of the former Middlemass Biscuit Factory. Photograph by Phyllis M. Cant.

After nibbling at the problem for some years the National Library acquired a building in Causewayside, previously occupied by the Middlemass Biscuit Factory. The Map

Library was housed there for several years, pending construction of a completely new building on the same site, to be erected in two phases. Design work on Phase I was started in 1980, construction began in 1984, and the building was in use by 1987. Design planning for Phase 2 began in 1988. Phase I was officially opened on 7th September 1989 by the Lord Chancellor, Lord Mackay of Clashfern. The building, designed by Andrew Merrylees Associates, is not without its critics, principally because its tall, angular towers and bright yellow staircases do not appear to be in harmony with adjacent buildings. Internally the building is a delight, both functionally and aesthetically. The arrangement of lifts, staircases and services, away from the main working areas, has created large uninterrupted floor space, where mobile bookstacks can be utilised to greatest advantage. The building is on seven levels, two of which, used for storage, are below ground level. Public access is at level 3 from Salisbury Place, leading to the Map Library at level 4 and the Scottish Science Library at level 5. Level 6 is used for storage and level 7 for staff accommodation.

The present Map Library has 1,250,000 maps, which are added to at the rate of 30,000 items annually. Although maps were first acquired by the Advocates' Library from about the middle of the eighteenth century, it was not until 1911 that an Act of Parliament confirmed that legal deposit definitely extended to maps and atlases. Once that was established the library's accessions increased greatly. The entire stock of maps from the Advocates' Library passed to the National Library of Scotland in 1925, but it was not until the 1950s that all the available material was extracted from the book collections. The first Map Room was established at George IV Bridge in 1958, greatly enhanced a decade later by 700,000 sheet maps acquired from the Ordnance Survey Record Store. The resultant acute shortage of space was not remedied until 1974 when the second Map Room was established in the Middlemass building, at Causewayside.

Lord Mackay of Clashfern, Lord High Chancellor of Great Britain, unveils the plaque to commemorate the opening of the First Phase of the National Library of Scotland's Causewayside Building on 7th September 1989. Photograph by Antonia Reeve. Courtesy of the Trustees of the National Library of Scotland.

Almost one million items were moved over a period of three months, prior to the official opening on 6th December 1974, by the President of the Royal Scottish Geographical Society. The third Map Room — subsequently renamed the Map Library — in the new Causewayside building was completed in 1987 with plan chests on mobile bases holding 1.5 million sheet maps, spacious desk accommodation for researchers, and a secure room for special collections.

The Map Library's total stock is breathtaking in volume and variety. Among the oldest manuscript maps are four of the twelfth, fourteenth and fifteenth centuries, depicting the known world at that time. Certain manuscript maps, which form an integral part of a collection of other papers, are held

211

H

by the Department of Manuscripts. Others, without accompanying papers, include maps of Scotland by Pont and Gordon, Adair, and a large stock of estate maps of the eighteenth and nineteenth centuries. The earliest printed map dates from 1472 and the earliest printed collection of maps is the 1478 edition of Claudius Ptolemy's *Cosmographia*, containing twenty-seven copperplate engraved maps, published in Rome. The earliest atlas is the 1592 edition of Abraham Ortelius's *Theatrum Orbis Terrarum*. There is also a large collection of early town maps, maps of the British Isles and the rest of the world. The special collections include: the Graham Brown Collection of Alpine maps and atlases bequeathed in 1965; the Marischal Collection of one hundred and thirty-seven maps covering the whole of Scotland between 1573 and 1873; the Newman Collection of books and maps covering every aspect of roads from the nineteenth century, presented by Professor Sydney Newman, Reid Professor of Music at the University of Edinburgh; and the Bartholomew Map Archive of most of the maps ever printed by John Bartholomew & Company and John Bartholomew & Son Ltd from 1877.

The Causewayside building also houses the Scottish Science Library opened in 1989 as a major advance in the provision of scientific and business information in Scotland. It has its origins in the 1970s when the National Library put forward proposals for the formation of a national science library. Around that time the Royal Society of Edinburgh was becoming increasingly concerned about the future of its own library of scientific books and papers. An obvious solution presented itself. In 1981 the Secretary of State for Scotland approved plans to form a new science library from the combined science resources of the National Library of Scotland and the Royal Society of Edinburgh.

The new library on the fifth floor of the Causewayside building has a fifty-seat reading area and space for approximately 144,000 volumes. The library receives four thousand current periodicals on science and business subjects and has

Dr Margaret Blackwood at Newington Library which was formally opened on 13th March 1975. Courtesy of *The Scotsman* Publications Ltd.

complete runs of *Science Abstracts* from 1898, *Chemical Abstracts* from 1907, *Biological Abstracts* from 1920 and *Science Citation Index* from 1945. The Scottish Business Information Service was inaugurated on 3rd November 1989.

NEWINGTON LIBRARY

WHILST NO ONE WOULD SUGGEST that the resources of Newington Library equal those of its close neighbour at Causewayside, nevertheless the branch library at Newington has fulfilled the public's expectations since it opened in 1975. Early in 1970 the Libraries and Museums Committee of Edinburgh Corporation was actively seeking a site for a branch library to serve the district of Newington. Possible sites at Duncan Street School and Relugas Road were considered, but rejected. In the following year, the Capital Investment

Programme made provision for a library to serve both Newington and Liberton, but, again, a suitable site could not be found to serve both communities equally. When the old Fountainhall Road Church site became vacant, the Corporation decided to build a library to serve Newington only, and a separate library was opened in September 1975 at Moredun.

After Fountainhall Road Church was demolished, work began on the new library, estimated to cost £167,000. Structural problems delayed progress by a few months, but the completed building was opened on 13th March 1975 by Councillor Robert Lorimer, Chairman of the Edinburgh Corporation Libraries and Museums Committee. The Rev. W. J. G. McDonald, Minister of Mayfield Church (later Moderator of the General Assembly of the Church of Scotland) was invited to participate in the service, emphasising the link with Fountainhall Road Church, whose congregation had united with Mayfield Church in 1958. The congregation of Mayfield Church presented a seat for the library forecourt and Mayfield Book Group gifted a watercolour painting, a woodland scene by Alexander S. Burns, 'given in memory of Helen Gunn M.A., by her friends'.

In many ways Newington Library was, and still is, revolutionary in the service it provides. Under its first librarian, Herbert Robertson, there was great emphasis on its being a community library and a centre for community-based activities for all ages, particularly through the local schools. Its most innovative service, however, was the introduction, for the first time in Edinburgh, of a Gramophone Record Library. In the first two months there were more than 10,000 record and tape issues and more than 60,000 book issues. The audio library issues rose to 103,000 during 1988~1989 and the book issues to almost one third of a million. The audio stock of 15,000 records and cassettes covers a wide range of tastes in music and other subjects. Of particular interest is the growing stock of talking books which are of great use, not only to the blind, but to those with partial sight or who have difficulty in holding a book for any length of time.

British Geological Survey

THE BRITISH GEOLOGICAL SURVEY moved to its new Scottish headquarters at South Park, Grange Terrace, in 1928. Prior to that the survey had occupied several buildings in Edinburgh during its long history.

The Geological Survey of Great Britain was established in 1835 with the principal aim of providing geological maps of the country, based on the Ordnance Survey maps, which were then becoming available. Its early years were understandably on a modest scale, despite the high calibre of its principal employees. For the first four years, H. T. De la Beche, Vice-President of the Geological Society, was the only geologist on the staff, and for the first two decades, surveys were mainly confined to the south of England. However, in the 1850s maps of Scotland with a scale 6″ to 1 mile began to be published, beginning with the Lothians. This enabled A. C. Ramsay to make a start, in 1854, to mapping the geology of the Dunbar area, a task which was later completed by H. H. Howell and Archibald Geikie. By 1859 most of Berwickshire, Lothians, Fife and Edinburgh had been completed and Geikie was able to provide geological information to assist James 'Paraffin' Young in his search for oil-shale deposits in West Lothian.

Meantime R. I. Murchison succeeded De la Beche as Director-General in 1855, a position which he held until his death in 1871, at age seventy-nine. Towards the end of his period in office, a Royal Commission recommended a large increase in staff, specifically to survey the national coal reserves in the north of Britain. This resulted in a complete reorganisation of the Survey in Scotland, which was given a separate identity, with headquarters in Edinburgh. A. Geikie was made Director, later assisted by his brother J. Geikie, as District Surveyor. In addition to his duties as Director, Archibald was appointed as the first Professor of Geology at Edinburgh University, the chair being founded by R. I. Murchison. When Archibald went to London in 1882 to

215

become Director-General, his brother James resigned from the Survey and succeeded him as Professor. Between them, the Geikies held the Chair for forty-three years.

In the twenty years from 1867 to 1887 substantial progress was made in surveying central and southern Scotland, but the speed of operations was noticeably slower when the Highlands were tackled. Despite extra staff being drafted in from England, a combination of poor weather, difficult terrain and more complicated geological problems resulted in a much slower rate of progress. However, towards the end of the century most of the Highlands had been completed and a start had been made to the islands of Skye and Raasay. The Orkney and Shetland Islands were not surveyed until very much later, in the late 1920s and early 1930s.

Coinciding with Geikie's retirement in 1901, two factors combined to alter dramatically the work being done by the Survey in Scotland. Another Royal Commission had found that the coalfield maps were out of date, necessitating the transfer of all available manpower to re-survey these areas of economic importance. A government committee had also been appointed to investigate several staffing problems, which appeared to have been ongoing since 1867! Its recommendations resulted in a restructuring and increase in staff. During the two World Wars, reduced resources were concentrated in areas of the greatest economic benefit, such as opencast coal mines and deposits of potash and mica.

The most important post-war administrative change took place in 1965 when the Survey's parent body (since 1919), the Department of Scientific and Industrial Research, ceased to exist. The Geological Survey of Great Britain was amalgamated with the Overseas Geological Surveys to form the Institute of Geological Sciences, under the control of the Natural Environment Research Council.

During its long history, the Survey has occupied several buildings in Edinburgh, some of which no longer exist. Between 1854 and 1867 geologists working in Scotland were

J. Horne, B. N. Peach and C. T. Clough in the field. Reproduced by permission of the Director, British Geological Survey: N.E.R.C. copyright reserved.

controlled from the London office. There was a temporary store for maps in the Industrial Museum of Scotland in Edinburgh, which changed its name to the Museum of Science and Art in 1864. The Survey remained at this Museum in Argyle Square until its demolition in 1869 to make way for the construction of the new museum in Chambers Street (now the Royal Museum of Scotland). The

Survey moved first to India Buildings in Victoria Street and then to offices in the then Sheriff Court building which stood on the site of the present National Library of Scotland in George IV Bridge. Cramped conditions led to a further move, in 1906, to a house at 33 George Square, previously occupied by Sir Noel Paton, the famous Scottish artist. South Park, in Grange Terrace, was acquired in 1928 and extended in 1931 and 1954. The final move was first mooted in 1964, to purpose-built accommodation, located at King's Buildings in 1967. Work began in 1971 and staff began to occupy the new building, Murchison House, in 1975. It was opened officially in 1977. The Survey retained South Park, which is occupied by staff dealing with offshore geology with particular reference to gas and oil resources.

More than one hundred and fifty years after its formation, the British Geological Survey still produces geological maps, but in recent years there has been a great increase in the scope of the work undertaken at Murchison House, South Park and other locations throughout the United Kingdom. This work includes many subjects which are a life's study in themselves: palaeontology, or the study of fossils, gathered from excavations, boreholes and natural exposure; mineralogy and petrology or the study of minerals and rocks, using a range of optical and x-ray facilities at Murchison House; and hydrogeology, or the study of geological factors relating to groundwater. Nowadays, the work of the Survey is by no means confined to the land, extensive offshore work being done to map the geology of the United Kingdom's continental shelf. The Department of Energy is also provided with information on the country's oil and gas resources, most of the work being done at South Park. Geomagnetism, or the study of the earth's magnetism, and seismology, the study of earthquakes, is also undertaken through a network of stations throughout the United Kingdom and abroad. A comprehensive enquiry service is available, backed by many years of practical experience, 120,000 volumes, 15,000 geology maps and a large collection

South Park in Grange Terrace acquired by the British Geological Survey in 1928 after occupying several sites in the Old Town of Edinburgh. Photograph by Phyllis M. Cant.

of photographs. Included in the collections of unpublished data are many borehole records and mining records, which are increasingly used to provide information for site investigation prior to various land and building developments.

A short history of the Survey, entitled *A History of the Geological Survey in Scotland*, by Dr R. B. Wilson was published in 1977.

NATURE CONSERVANCY COUNCIL

HOPE TERRACE, and similar streets to the west of Kilgraston Road, are generally considered to be part of the modern district of Grange: historically they were built on the estate of Whitehouse, which lay between the Grange estate and the smaller estates of Greenhill and East Morningside. No. 12

Hope Terrace, a beautifully restored building set in a large feu of ground, has been owned by the Nature Conservancy Council since 1950.

The house was built in 1854 for Benjamin Hall Blyth, who gave it the name Braeside. Blyth was the founder of the family firm of Blyth, Civil Engineers of No. 135 George Street, Edinburgh. He was born in 1819, the son of Robert Brittain Blyth, and was apprenticed to Mr Miller of Grainger and Miller, who were engaged in the construction of railways for the North British Railway, the Northern Railway and the Kilmarnock to Carlisle Railway. In 1848, when the last partner retired, he offered the firm to Blyth and three other associates, but Blyth decided to set up in business on his own. After a slow start he was successful in bidding for the construction of the Slamannan to Bo'ness line, which led to many other contracts in Scotland and in England. In 1854 he took his younger brother, Edward, as a partner in the firm B. & E. Blyth, but Benjamin had worked himself into ill-health and died in 1866 at the age of only forty-seven. Despite this loss, the firm went from strength to strength under several names, but always including the family name of the founder. Benjamin Hall Blyth (the second), son of the founder, was taken into the firm in 1871, which continued to be involved in the construction of major railways and stations, including the Waverley. They were also involved in the construction of the Broomielaw Bridge over the Clyde and the New North Bridge in Edinburgh. In 1909 Benjamin Hall Blyth (the third), grandson of the founder, joined the firm and worked on one of the largest contracts, Methil Dock in Fife. During the First World War, Blyth held the rank of Colonel in the Royal Engineers working principally in France. Post-First World War contracts included coal railways in East Lothian, the Scottish Rugby Union stadium at Murrayfield in 1925, and the Kirkcaldy and Musselburgh Sea Walls. At the centenary in 1948 a short history of the firm, *One Hundred Years*, was compiled. At the present day the firm

Benjamin Hall Blyth
Founder of the Firm
(1819-1866).

Benjamin Hall Blyth
Past President of the Institution
of Civil Engineers, Son of the
Founder (1849-1917).

Benjamin Hall Blyth
Ex-Lord Dean of Guild of the City
of Edinburgh, Grandson of the
Founder and Present Senior Partner.

Three generations of Blyth and Blyth — with much in common. From *One Hundred Years*, courtesy of the Blyth and Blyth Group.

operates as the Blyth & Blyth Group but no member of the Blyth family holds office.

After Benjamin Hall Blyth (the first) died in 1866 his widow remained at Hope Terrace for only a short time. The property was then occupied by Baron Grahame of Morphie and subsequently by David Deuchar in 1880, who lived there until his death in 1904. David Deuchar was an actuary by profession and entered the Standard Life Assurance Company at the age of fifteen, later transferring to the Caledonian Insurance Company where he became General Manager in 1875.

In more recent years the house at No. 12 Hope Terrace (renamed Harlaw around 1911) was the family home of John Paterson-Brown, silk mercer, of Edinburgh who took occupation in 1920 and owned the house twice between then and 1943. When his son Keith Paterson-Brown M.B.,

F.R.C.S. Ed. married Margaret Cleland Wishart in 1922 they also lived for a few years at Harlaw. Keith was born in Edinburgh in 1893 and was educated at Merchiston Castle School and Edinburgh University, where he graduated in 1916. Thereafter, he served in the Royal Army Medical Corps in Mesopotamia, Persia and the Caucasus until the end of the First World War. On returning to Edinburgh he was elected to the fellowship of the Royal College of Surgeons in 1921 and spent most of his working life as a surgeon to the Royal Infirmary of Edinburgh. When he retired in 1958 he was senior surgeon to the Infirmary and visiting surgeon to the Princess Margaret Rose Hospital and Roodlands Hospital. He died in 1982 at the age of eighty-eight survived by two sons (one of whom is in medical practice in the Borders), and six grandchildren, two of whom have subsequently qualified in medicine.

Shortly after the death of J. Paterson-Brown, silk mercer, in 1943 Harlaw was renamed Lydele, when it was the home of Baron Georges E. E. Marchand of the French Consulate in Edinburgh.

The architect's original drawings for Harlaw have not been traced, but alterations were made by David Deuchar in 1891. He built a billiard room on the south-east gable and added a porch over the front doorway, the drawings for which show ornate stonework, incorporating the letter D, on either side of the entrance. In 1928, when the house was owned by a Mrs Margaret Buist, the billiard room was converted into a day nursery and various alterations were made to other apartments. The detailed plans provide an excellent example of how the interior of a large family house in the Grange was organised in the late 1920s. There were three main floors: the basement included the maid's room, servants' hall, kitchen, the cook's bedroom and separate small rooms for wine, sticks, coals and the washhouse; the first floor contained the library, dining room, principal bedroom, servants' bedroom and pantry; and the first floor was occupied by five bedrooms and a large drawing room on the south-west corner of the house. In 1950 the house was

Harlaw in Hope Terrace occupied by the Nature Conservancy Council since 1950, formerly the house of Benjamin Hall Blyth. Courtesy of the Nature Conservancy Council.

purchased for the sum of £8500 by the Nature Conservancy Council as its headquarters for Scotland. In recent years the entire building has been beautifully restored and Deuchar's billiard room is presently occupied by the Map Department.

The Nature Conservancy Council is the Government agency responsible for nature conservancy throughout Britain. In that capacity it provides advice to the Government, and others, on all matters relating to nature conservation. It also has the essentially practical task of selecting, establishing and managing a series of National Nature Reserves and Sites of Special Scientific Interests throughout the country. The framework in which the Council operates was greatly extended and strengthened in 1981 by the Wildlife and Countryside Act. In Scotland, the Council has four regional offices at Riccarton near Edinburgh, Balloch, Aberdeen and

Inverness, and eighteen smaller sub-regional offices from Lerwick in the Shetlands to Dalbeattie in Dumfries and Galloway.

The need for nature conservation in Scotland, and elsewhere, has never been greater: there has been a phenomenal increase in the rate of destruction of the natural world, witness the continuing destruction of the equatorial rain forests; environmental pollution has reached worrying levels; and the misuse of resources has resulted in con- siderable waste. Despite its relatively small geographical area in world terms, Scotland is of particular importance in many areas of nature conservation. Its cool, moist climate encourages many ferns, mosses and lichens, and its bird fauna is particularly important, both for its resident species and winter refuge visitors. The sparse human population over large tracts of Scotland does, of course, enhance the value of many mountain, moorland and peat-bog sites of national and international importance. Whilst the Council regards all areas of conservation as important, special attention is given to two main areas, Sites of Special Scientific Interests (SSSI's) and National Nature Reserves (NNR's).

There are 1400 SSSI's in Scotland. Under the 1981 Act the Nature Conservancy Council has a statutory duty to notify these sites, especially if they are endangered. The manner in which the sites are selected and notified often involves lengthy research and protracted consultation with other land-use interests. Initially a broad survey of the intended area is carried out and all relevant published research and reports are brought together, so that the overall picture can be seen. That is followed by a much more detailed investigation of the site, in consultation with the landowner. Exact boundaries are established and, after social and economic factors are considered, a decision is taken by the Council on whether or not to select that area. If approved, the site is notified to the various interested parties, and objections are considered. After selection and notification, the most suitable management plan is drawn up, having regard to existing and future land-use.

There are far fewer National Nature Reserves: sixty-eight in Scotland. They are frequently of larger geographical area than SSSI's and usually concentrate on the protection of the specific features for which they were designated. In some Reserves, such as Beinn Eighe or Creag Meagaidh, the public are encouraged to visit, and educational and interpretive aids, such as information points, nature trails and leaflets are made available.

No one would suggest that the work of the Nature Conservancy Council is without its areas of potential conflict. These are chiefly associated with the social and economic uses to which the land is already put. In addition there is potential conflict in at least two unexpected areas, namely agriculture and forestry. Fortunately, close consultation between the Council and the Scottish Agriculture Colleges and Forestry Commission has reduced these areas of potential conflict to a minimum. Reclamation and drainage of moorlands and peatlands for agriculture has greatly reduced their wildlife value, and there has been recent concern at the growth of coniferous afforestation on traditional hill pasture. Of particular interest is the proposal, welcomed by the Council, to establish a 'Central Scotland Forest' between Edinburgh and Glasgow with plantings of native coniferous and deciduous species.

The Council is also involved in the protection of the freshwater environment, marine conservation, and providing advice to the Crown Estate Commissioners on the control and allocation of sites for fish farms.

THE SALVATION ARMY

THE SALVATION ARMY has had a significant presence in the Grange since 1935 when it purchased a large detached house, known as Blackford Park, at No. 29 South Oswald Road.

Blackford Park was built around 1871 for Andrew Usher of Andrew Usher & Co., Distillers, who had their premises at Sciennes Street. Andrew was born in 1826, in West Nicolson Street, one of fourteen children of Andrew Usher,

Snr., the founder of the brewing and distilling business. With his brother John, Andrew Jnr. entered the family business where he combined his natural energy with a measure of eccentricity. It is said that during business hours he avoided all verbal communication with his brother, resorting to the rather formal practice of sending written notes, sometimes about the most mundane aspects of the business. In *A History of the Usher Family in Scotland* the authors recount that on one occasion Andrew wrote to his brother, before their usual amicable lunch meeting, saying: 'Although I have allowed your son, Robert, to lunch with us, I wish it to be understood that he must not speak unless his opinion is asked. Yesterday he spoke several times when he had no right to do so'. Through hard work and shrewd business dealings Andrew amassed considerable wealth in his own lifetime. He gifted the sum of £100,000 in 1896 for the construction of a 'City Hall to seat 3,000, the exterior of which was to be dignified and simple'. He died on 1st November 1898 at the age of seventy-two and was buried on 4th November 1898 in the south-west corner of Grange Cemetery, beside his first wife and four of his children who had predeceased him. He was married twice, firstly in 1854 to Elizabeth Langmuir Miller, who died in 1876, and then, in 1879, to Marion Blackwood Murray who died in 1925. Of the many biographical notes on Andrew Usher, perhaps that from his son-in-law Gordon Burn-Murdoch is nearest the mark:

> He was thin hard, not an ounce of fat. Head like a Caesar, but finer, clean cut between a Caesar and Pharaoh, very good, quiet carriage, in fact distinguished very much so, but in a very unostentatious manner'. . .

Sadly, Andrew Usher did not see the completed 'City Hall' which later bore his name. After much delay in the choice of an appropriate site, the Usher Hall, designed by J. Stockdale Harrison of Leicester, was built on an angular site to the east of Lothian Road. Two memorial stones were laid by King

Blackford Park built around 1871 for Andrew Usher of Andrew Usher & Co., Distillers who gifted £100,000 for the construction of 'a City Hall to seat 3,000'. Blackford Park was bought by the Salvation Army in 1935 and demolished in 1982. Courtesy of the Royal Commission on the Ancient and Historical Monuments of Scotland.

George V and Queen Mary on 19th July 1911, and the hall was officially opened by Andrew's widow on 6th March 1914.

Blackford Park, in which Andrew Usher spent the latter part of his life, was a magnificent stone dwelling of two main storeys and an attic floor, with four principal rooms, a billiard room and eleven bedrooms, in addition to the kitchens and other offices. Its south-facing rear elevation was designed to take maximum advantage of its elevated position looking towards Blackford Hill. Andrew lived there from 1871 until his death in 1898, after which Mrs Usher remained in the family home until 1920. Shortly thereafter, the property was acquired by Miss Dick and Miss Saunders who used the extensive accommodation as Canaan School for Girls, formerly Canaan Park College in the grounds of the Astley

Ainslie Hospital. As the school roll increased, the proprietors set up an annexe in 1925 in the adjacent property, Carrington House, at No. 27 South Oswald Road. In 1935 Blackford Park was sold to the Salvation Army.

The acquisition of Blackford Park was handled by John Baird, solicitor to the Salvation Army, and concluded at Dowell's Rooms in George Street. The house, intended for fifty residents, and renamed Sunnyside, was officially opened on 16th October 1935 by Mrs Bramwell Booth (daughter-in-law of William Booth the founder of the Salvation Army), at a ceremony presided over by Lord Salvesen. Sunnyside continued to provide comfortable surroundings for many residents until the late 1970s when the state of repair of the house and the cost of maintaining it reached a critical stage. A decision was taken to demolish the house, despite efforts by the Cockburn Association to save it. It was completely demolished in 1982, the valuable stone and slate being small compensation for the loss of such a fine building. The lodge house was saved and is still extant. A few artefacts remain, mainly from the exterior stonework, which are now displayed in the garden ground of the new complex, beside the stone lion from the original entrance. Internally, the only feature believed to relate to the Usher family was a group of relief plaster mouldings which was set into the wall of the vestibule. The centre moulding contained a relief medallion of a male, and a female, head. The outer mouldings depicted, on the left, a scene showing picking of grapes, and, on the right, trampling the grapes in a large tub. During demolition, the workmen came across a rather curious brick-lined cavity, beneath the entrance driveway, which contained a number of wires. Further investigation revealed that the wires ran from the kitchen quarters on the east side of the house to the tradesmen's entrance at the west side. The cavity was still dry and clear of debris, and when the wires were tightened the kitchen bells rang clearly. It is not known how old the mechanism was but its existence suggests that security was important, and that free access to the house was not available from the street.

Prior to demolition of the old house, the Salvation Army had already planned an extensive redevelopment of the site. Existing residents were moved from Sunnyside to the new Eventide Home built on the north side of the extensive grounds. When the house was demolished the remainder of the complex was built to provide a variety of sheltered and independent flats for elderly single and married persons. A substantial part of the south feu was sold separately for private housing development.

BARNARDO'S

BLACKFORD BRAE, in South Oswald Road, has been owned and occupied by Barnardo's as a residential home since 1945. Like Blackford Park to the east, its history dates from the early 1870s.

On 28th July 1871 Richard Trotter granted a feu charter of over two acres of land to James Cuthbertson Cunningham, Linseed Manufacturer of Leith, on condition that the house to be erected would have a value of not less than £3,000. Trotter's signature on the very lengthy document is witnessed by 'Charles Moss my Butler and John Milne my Footman'. The completed house was a very grand three-storey building in the Scottish baronial style with numerous crowsteps and pediments, set in extensive grounds running down to the Jordan Burn. Mr Cunningham remained in the house until around 1881, after which it was owned by several prominent businessmen in Edinburgh including W. S. Davidson, General Manager of the New Zealand and Australian Land Co. Ltd., and C. A. Stitt of Broughton Soap Works. From 1932 to 1944 Blackford Brae was the home of Sir Thomas Henry Holland, Principal and Vice-Chancellor of Edinburgh University, whose numerous public appointments are listed at length in *Who Was Who 1941–1950*. The house was bought by Dr Barnardo's Homes in 1945 for the sum of £6,000, and was recently renumbered from No. 31 to No. 91 South Oswald Road.

Throughout the world the name Barnardo is synonymous with the care and protection of children. Despite detailed research, the early life of the founder and his first years in London are not fully known. On 1st January 1827 John Michaelis Barnardo, a furrier in Dublin, married Elizabeth O'Brien, who bore him six children, but died giving birth to their seventh child in August 1836. The following year, John married Elizabeth's sister, Abigail, the union being solemnised in a German Church in London as marriage to a sister of a deceased's wife was still illegal in Dublin. On 4th July 1845 Abigail gave birth to her fourth son, Thomas John Barnardo, who was educated at St. Patrick's Cathedral Grammar School, and later went to work in the wine trade in Dublin. Thomas showed little or no inclination towards a religious or caring life in his youth, but gradually he became less opposed to the mass evangelical meetings attended by his mother. Although his dislike of mass meetings never waned, he warmed to the atmosphere of smaller, more personal, meetings where he underwent a 'conversion'. He began to work with the poor in the slums of Dublin and later went to London in 1866. He settled in the East End shortly before the devastating cholera epidemic in Stepney which claimed many thousands of lives. His first small lodging house for children was at 18 Stepney Causeway.

Barnardo's was not established in Scotland until the end of the Second World War. The headquarters are at Corstorphine Road, in Edinburgh, and there are child care projects in Central, Strathclyde, Lothian and Tayside Regions. Funding is from a combination of Local Authority Grants, legacies, industrial appeals, and the proceeds of Barnardo shops and house-to-house collections. Barnardo's work independently from, but in liaison with, Social Work and Education Departments and Health Boards. Over the years they have moved away from a predominantly residential emphasis to include day-care provision, family placement, and work with youngsters leaving care. Of eighteen projects currently operating in Scotland six are residential, one of

Blackford Brae in South Oswald Road was built in the early 1870s for James Cuthbertson Cunningham, Linseed Manufacturers of Leith. It has been a residential house for Barnardo's since 1945. Courtesy of Barnardo's Scotland.

which is at No. 91 South Oswald Road (Blackford Brae). The house has a capacity of sixteen children although the usual number is nearer twelve — always more boys than girls — between the ages of five and thirteen. Currently a short-time stay of up to two years is offered, to provide a safe environment and a regular routine away from the background in which the problem arose. There is at the same time emphasis on helping the family, so that wherever possible the child will be able to return to his or her own home. In the near future, further developments are envisaged. The building will become a day special school for up to twenty-four primary age children. About half will attend from their own homes, and half will be cared for in two normal-sized houses in the community. Again, the project will work closely with children and families to enable

231

youngsters to be reintegrated into their own families, neighbourhoods and schools, wherever possible.

GLENBOURNE

GLENBOURNE was built around 1870 on the north side of South Oswald Road within a few hundred yards of the feus on which Blackford Park and Blackford Brae were built. The house was named Glenbourne in 1874 by the second occupier, John MacFarlane, Justice of the Peace, who lived there until around 1904. Shortly thereafter the house was owned by James Allan, M.A., Classics Master at George Watson's College. James Allan, born in Banffshire in 1863, was educated at Keith Grammar School and King's College, Aberdeen, before taking up his first teaching post as Classical Master of the Grammar School at Aberystwyth. He joined the staff of Watson's in 1888 and remained there for forty years, retiring in 1928 as head of the Classics Department. In addition to his teaching responsibilities he and his wife ran one of Watson's many small boarding houses, first at No. 25 George Square and then at Glenbourne. He died in 1943 a few weeks short of his eightieth birthday.

After the Second World War, Glenbourne was acquired by Edinburgh University and used by various departments including the Animal Breeding Research Organisation and later the Seismology Research Unit. It is at present occupied by the Scottish Agricultural College, field workers from the Lothians Agricultural Advisory Service and part of the Edinburgh School of Agriculture which has its headquarters at King's Buildings in West Mains Road.

SUGGESTIONS FOR FURTHER READING

Author	Title and Year of Publication (in brackets)
Anderson, Malcolm	The Reid Memorial Church Edinburgh – A Jubilee Description 1935-1985 (1986)
Anderson, William Pitcairn	Silences That Speak (1931)
Ballingall, William	Edinburgh Past and Present (1877)
Blyth & Blyth	One Hundred Years – A History of Blyth & Blyth 1848-1948 (1948)
Bradley, O. Charnock	History of the Edinburgh Veterinary College (1923)
Campion, Mary	Place of Springs (1977)
Cant, Malcolm	Marchmont in Edinburgh (1984)
Cockburn, Lord	Memorials of His Time (1910)
Craig, W. S.	Royal Hospital for Sick Children, Edinburgh 1895-1970 (1970)
Daiches, David	Two Worlds (1956)
Daiches, Jones & Jones (Editors)	A Hotbed of Genius (1986)
Dick-Lauder, Sir Thomas	Scottish Rivers (1874)
Downie, Hay	Fifty Years at 'Argyle Place' 1927-1977 (1977)
Dunlop, Rev. A. Ian	The Kirks of Edinburgh (1988)
Finlayson, Charles P.	Clement Litill and His Library (1980)
Forbes, T.	A Brief History of Newington South Church 1848-1948 (1948)
Gibb, Graham L.	Horatius Bonar and His Hymns (1989)

Gibson, Thomas	Argyle Place United Free Church Edinburgh 1877-1927 (1927)
Gifford, McWilliam & Walker	The Buildings of Scotland — Edinburgh (1984)
Gladstone, J. W. E.	Warrender Church 1886-1936 (1936)
Goodfellow, James	The Print of His Shoe (1906)
Grange Association	The Grange — A Case for Conservation (1982)
Grant, James	Old & New Edinburgh (1882)
Gray, John G.	The South Side Story (1962)
Guthrie, Douglas	The Royal Edinburgh Hospital for Sick Children 1860-1960 (1960)

A History of the Usher Family in Scotland (1956)

Hunter, D. L. G.	Edinburgh's Transport (1964)
Keir, David	The Younger Centuries 1749-1949 (1951)
Lee, Miss C. Fraser	The Real St. Trinnean's (1962)

The Lord Provosts of Edinburgh (1932)

MacGregor, Alasdair Alpin	Auld Reekie (1943)
MacGregor, Alasdair Alpin	The Turbulent Years (1945)
MacGregor, Alasdair Alpin	The Golden Lamp (1964)
Maxwell, Thomas	St. Catherine's in Grange Church 1866-1966 (1966)
Mayfield U. F. Church	Mayfield United Free Church 1875-1925 (1925)
Mayfield and Fountainhall Church	Mayfield and Fountainhall (1962)
Moffat, J. A. R. (Editor)	Mayfield 100 (1975)

Newington United Presbyterian Church Jubilee Memorial 1848-1898 (1898)

Phillips, Abel	A History of the Origins of the First Jewish Community in Scotland — Edinburgh 1816 (1979)
Pringle, James	The Story of West St. Giles Church 1699-1916 (1916)
Royal Commission on the Ancient Monuments of Scotland	The City of Edinburgh (1951)
Searle, Ronald	The St. Trinian's Story (1959)
Seton, George	The Convent of Saint Catherine of Sienna (1871)

SUGGESTIONS FOR FURTHER READING

Smith, Charles J.	Historic South Edinburgh, four volumes (1978, 1979, 1986, 1988)
Smith, Charles J.	South Edinburgh in Pictures (1989)
Smith, Mrs J. Stewart	The Grange of St. Giles (1897)
Stevenson, Dr N. L.	Play (1946)
Storer, J. & H. S.	Views of Edinburgh (1820)
Thomson, Leslie G.	The Reid Memorial Church (1934)
various	Book of the Old Edinburgh Club (1908 to date)
Walker, J. J.	Fountainhall Road Church, Edinburgh: History of the Congregation (1929)

Whitehouse & Grange Bowling Club 1872-1972   (1972)

Wilson, Sir Daniel	Memorials of Edinburgh in the Olden Time (1891)
Wilson, Dr R. B.	A History of the Geological Survey in Scotland (1977)
	Newington United Presbyterian Church Jubilee Memorial 1848-1898 (1898)
	The Lord Provosts of Edinburgh (1932)
	A History of the Usher Family in Scotland (1956)
	Whitehouse & Grange Bowling Club 1872-1972 (1972)

INDEX

Edinburgh Hospital for
  Incurables 180
Edinburgh Southern Institution
  152
Egremont 148
Esdaile 139
Esdaile Old Girls Union 146

Ferguson, Prof. Adam 48
Foot, Victorine 59
Fountainhall Road Church 125,
  214

Gayfield House 196
George Watson's College 205
George Watson's Ladies' College
  205
German Lutheran Church 130
Gladstone Terrace 68, 74
Glenbourne 232
Gowans, Sir James 90
Grainger & Miller Feuing Plan 80
Grange Association 8
Grange Cemetery 22, 91
Grange Church 106
Grange Cricket Club 96
Grange Estate Plan 78
Grange Farm 47, 74, 82
Grange Home School 157
Grange House 1, 11, 22
Grange Park House 148

Highland & Agricultural Society
  192
Hope Park Church 121
Hope, Thomas of Rankeiller 46

Jewish Burial Ground 52
Johnstone, Sir James 43, 66
Johnstone, Sir William 32, 47

Kilravock 184
Kininmonth, William 91
Kinross, John 90

Lauder, Sir Andrew 17
Lee, Miss C. Fraser 154
Litill, Clement 42
Little Company of Mary 185
Livingstone Place 74
Longmore Hospital 180
Longmore, J. A., W.S. 181
Lyon, Hermon 52

MacGregor, Alasdair Alpin 77
Mackay, Lord of Clashfern 210
McMath, Janet 14, 16, 38
Marchmont St. Giles Church 105
Mayfield Church 125
Mayfield North Church 126
Meadow Place 56
Meadowside House 173
Melville Drive 76
Miller, George 69
Ministers' Daughters' College 142
Monk's Seat 26
Monkwood 8
Morham, Robert 86, 108
Morley Smith, Mrs Edith 158
Morley Smith, Miss Joan 159
Mount Grange 8
Murchison, Prof. R. I. 215
Mureburgh 35

National Library of Scotland
  207
Nature Conservancy Council 219
New Campbeltown 34, 55
Newington Library 213
Newington South Church 122